TABLE OF CONTENTS

Page

ACRONYMS

CCP   Chinese Communist Party

IEA   Islamic Emirate of Afghanistan

ISI   Inter-Service Intelligence

KMT   Kuomintang

US   United States

CHAPTER 1

INTRODUCTION

Background

The Chinese Communist Party (CCP) provided Mao a means to implement his revolutionary ideas. Mao Tse Tung managed to execute his revolutionary agenda successfully. Through his various selected works, one could see how the strategy of his revolutionary movement evolved. Using classical Marxism and some elements of Leninism as his baseline, Mao modified the ideology to fit conditions in China. Mao's ideas on conducting protracted war also revealed issues he had to face when mobilizing forces, building popular support for the CCP, and gaining power of the central government in the process. Mao also wrote about problems in executing guerrilla warfare against both the Kuomintang (KMT) as well as the Imperial Japanese invasion. Mao's writings and actions provided examples and explanations as to what led to his success.

The research examined various issues Mao faced in gaining popular support for the CCP during the Chinese Civil War. These issues dealt mostly with maintaining cohesion within the CCP long enough to achieve strategic success through protracted war. The study further determined whether these same issues apply to the Taliban's attempts to regain control of Afghanistan, and establish its Islamic Emirate of Afghanistan (IEA). Knowing whether similar issues existed between Mao's and the Taliban movements revealed possible vulnerabilities in the Taliban's strategy.

Revolution is a ―major, sudden, and hence typically violent alteration in government and in related associations and structures."[1] This action is a human solution. For this reason, revolutionary strategies have vulnerabilities in their design. Therefore, each action in a revolutionary movement is a calculated one and ideally linked with an overarching ideology and supporting strategy. Without the presence of a well thought-out strategy, it is unlikely a revolutionary movement can reach its envisioned endstate.

The Research Question

The research topic used the Maoist revolutionary approach to examine the Taliban's current strategy, and gain insights on the movements suggested vulnerabilities. Several questions needed to be answered to understand historical context behind the formation of each revolutionary strategy. The primary question addressed was: ―Could Mao's revolutionary approach even be compared to the Taliban's strategy?" This required a close examination of both movements' ideologies and the motivations of both leaders. These movements' historical similarities validated whether the research study was viable.

Once the backgrounds were checked and deemed comparable, this study led to the second primary question: ―What were the fundamentals of Mao's revolutionary approach?" The study examined the relevant fundamentals of Maoism by referencing his *Selected Works* dealing with revolution. The study defined what the Taliban's strategy

---

[1] *The New Encyclopedia Britannica,* 15th ed., s.v. ―revolution."

was from its rise in 1996 up to the present day using recent events.[2] The Taliban's strategy was superimposed over the Maoist revolutionary approach to gain insights on vulnerabilities.

Comparison of both strategies distinguished whether common fundamentals existed between the CCP's and the Taliban's strategy. This led the researcher to answer the secondary questions: "What were the commonalities in terms of history, ideology and components in each revolutionary strategy?" as well as "What did Mao's revolutionary approach have that Taliban did not?" After these secondary actions were answered, they all merged to answer the research question.

Chapter Overviews

The Literature Review presented the major works which influenced and shaped Mao. The second section provided an overview on some of Mao's central *Selected Works*. These selected works described the theory that made up the core of Mao's revolutionary approach. These features covered the roles peasants had as part of the CCP, and works that expressed Mao's anti-imperialistic views. The third section introduced indispensible references that aided in understanding Mao's revolutionary approach. Secondary sources were part of the fourth section which elaborated on the conditions leading to Maoism, as well as sources that discussed Mao's political methods to maintain a tolerable level of mass-mobilization. The last section listed key sources on understanding the Taliban's strategy and its desired outcomes.

---

[2]Neamatollah Nojumi, *The Rise of the Taliban in Afghanistan, Mass Mobilization, Civil War, and the Future of the Region* (New York: Palgrave, 2002), Chronology of Events.

The methodology in chapter 3 explained the approach that was used to answer the research question. The research first required a clear understanding of Maoism and how it was derived from Marxist-Leninism. The next phase discussed the Taliban's history, ideology, and general strategy. The histories and ideologies were both compared for similarities, and validated the legitimacy of the research. The next phase of the study required superimposing Mao's protracted war strategy onto the Taliban's strategy to gain insights on potential vulnerabilities.

The Analysis and Interpretation of Evidence in chapter 4 provided a comprehensive explanation of Maoism and explored the historical context that led Mao to adopt Marxist-Leninism. In this chapter the author compared both movements' histories, ideologies, and revolutionary actions. The collected vulnerabilities concentrated on how mass mobilization was affected by the original movement's ideology. The research also found how mass mobilization was crucial to Mao's protracted war strategy. This suggested that the concept of mass mobilization may have been just as important to the Taliban's movement as well.

The conclusion in chapter 5 summarized the research and provided overall findings. The research showed that mass mobilization was the primary vulnerability to Mao's success. Mao succeeded in maintaining mobilization of his army. It was determined his success was attributed to a well designed protracted war strategy. Applying the protracted war strategy to the Taliban revealed three insights. These insights dealt with the role ideology had in maintaining mass mobilization, the garnering of international support, and the problems behind maintaining cohesion.

Definitions

Bourgeoisie is used in Marxist thought and is the class of society that owns the most important means of production, through which it exploits the working class.[3]

Caliphate (*Khelafat*) is the system of government established in Islam and represented the political unity of the Muslim nation.[4]

Comprador is also a member of the Chinese merchant class who aided Western traders in China in the late 19th and early 20th centuries. The term has come to denote those people who aided Western exploitation of China.[5]

Dialectic Materialism is concerned with the growth of the consciousness of man in society and not with the unfolding consciousness of the ―world spirit."[6]

Proletariat is the class of modern wage laborers who having no means of production of their own, are reduced to selling their labor power in order to live.[7]

Sharia is the body of knowledge used by Islamic scholars and lawyers in the various schools of jurisprudence that have emerged since the emergence of Islam.[8]

---

[3]Steven Cahn, *Classics of Political and Moral Philosophy* (New York: Oxford, 2002), 865.

[4]*The New Encyclopedia Britannica*, 15th ed., s.v. ―caliphate."

[5]*The New Encyclopedia Britannica*, 15th ed., s.v. ―comprador."

[6]*The Blackwell Dictionary of Political Science,* s.v. ―dialectical materialism," http://www.netlibrary.com/reader/ (accessed May 23, 2011).

[7]Cahn, *Classics of Political and Moral Philosophy*, 865

[8]Abdul Salaam Zaeef, *My Life With the Taliban* (New York: Columbia University Press, 2010), 305.

Vanguard is the elite party cadre which according to Lenin, would be used to organize the masses as a revolutionary force and give effect to Communist planning.[9]

Scope

The research concentrated on two particular periods. The first period covered the time between the 1911 Chinese Revolution up to the point Mao began writing his foundational essays on Communism in the late 1930s.[10] The second period went from the start of the Chinese Civil War to the start of the 1937 Imperial Japanese Invasion. This period encompassed Mao's validation of protracted war principles. Mao emphasized through his works, the role of mass mobilization when fighting against imperialist aggressors. The period between 1911 to 1937 was easiest to superimpose on the Taliban's history and current efforts to regain power.

The research is a comparative political analysis, and evaluated the ideas of the Taliban and how they were applied against the CCP. The author did not delve into military tactics of protracted war, but looked at its purpose in a political context. As a result, the study transformed into a philosophical and populist one. The author revealed how irrelevant a military vulnerability was in revolutionary approaches as long as mass mobilization and self preservation were maintained. From the conclusions, the author determined military action was a tool to orchestrate a larger plan to isolate the enemy politically.

---

[9] *Oxford English Dictionary* 2d ed., s.v. "vanguard."

[10] Mao wrote "On Practice" and "On Contradiction" in 1937, "Dialectical Materialism" in 1938.

6

Importance of the Study

The author revealed insights on Taliban vulnerabilities using purely Maoist theories. It provided a different perspective on how the Taliban executed their strategy. The author also revealed a different way to look at insurgency and revolutionary action in comparison to Western versions of insurgency. I also looked for elements of universality in revolutionary approaches. The research supported the claim that revolutionary movements had similar functioning actions and characteristics that went beyond culture and time period.

Another importance was finding out how the formation of ideology could either benefit or detriment efforts to achieve victory by revolution. From the research, it was determined that ideology defined and selected the target audience to conduct revolutionary movement. The segment of population picked affected the strategy. Based on the research, I suggest that in developing an ideology it was important to foresee the receptiveness of it and determine whether it appealed to a majority of the population the leader wanted to influence.

The author attempted to look for any vulnerabilities in the Taliban strategy to suggest a method to counter them using an enemy-centric approach. The United States' (US) current counterinsurgency doctrine is population-centric. The *Counterinsurgency 3-24* goes over all the various elements that make up an insurgency, but does not direct planners to procedurally formulate the enemy's strategy and objectives. With this research, I attempted to conduct an enemy focused analysis of the strategies to pinpoint vulnerabilities relevant to the leader of the insurgency.

CHAPTER 2

LITERATURE REVIEW

Works Which Influenced Mao

Chinese literature and commentary heavily shaped Mao's views on the causes and effects of Western influence prior to being exposed to the *Communist Manifesto* and accepting basic Marxism as his worldview.[11] During the period of Chinese instability, there were several viewpoints on the effects of western influence. Scholars like T'an Ssu-t'ung believed that the invasion of foreign powers —rid the country of what was rotten and illegitimate" within the government.[12] Others such as Ch'en Tu-hsiu believed that —China's misfortune resulted largely from her own weaknesses, and could be cured by learning from the West."[13] Classics such as *Romance of the Three Kingdoms* and *Water Margin* inspired Mao's militaristic thinking heavily and his vision to reunite the Chinese back to its revered status. These works highlighted the warrior-stateman, and heroic bandits that took from the oppressive rich and helped the victimized poor. These were familiar figures, he sought to emulate.[14]

Mao also explored contemporary Western ideologies. Karl Marx, Fredrick Engels, and Vladimir Lenin influenced Mao deeply. Mao indicated this influence by referring to Lenin's work *What is to be Done?* and *Conspectus of Hegel's Science of Logic* while

---

[11]Stuart R. Schram, *The Political Thought of Mao Tse Tung* (New York: Praeger, 1969), 35. Mao dates his conversion to Marxism only from the winter of 1919-1920.

[12]Ibid.,19.

[13]Ibid.

[14]Ibid.,23.

8

writing *On Practice*. Mao referred to Marx's *Introduction of Political Economy and Engel's Dialectics, Quantity and Quality* in his concepts of contradiction.[15] Lenin's arguments in particular helped inspire Mao to extend the Communist revolution into China. For Lenin the Communist world revolution could escape its Eurocentrism and travel into Asia.[16] Yet in order to accomplish this, Mao had to determine the most effective societal arrangement to execute revolution in an underdeveloped country like China. At the same time the revolution needed to maintain fundamentals of Marx's ideology. Mao's *Selected Works* presented his solution to this problem, and is now referred to as Maoism.

Mao Selected Works

One journal article that led me to Mao's works on insurgency and protracted warfare was Edward L. Katzenbach's article "The Revolutionary Strategy of Mao Tse-Tung."[17] Katzenbach provided several footnotes on additional resources like Mao's *Selected Works*. Mao has a collection of translated essays entitled *Selected Works of Mao Tse-Tung*. The collection consisted of ten volumes of Mao's essays. Mao wrote his works

---

[15]Mao Tse Tung, "On Contradiction," in *Selected Works of Mao Tse Tung* (Peking: Foreign Languages Press, 1967), 1:346-347. Endnotes refer to all these works from Lenin, Marx, and Engel.

[16]Schram, *The Political Thought of Mao Tse Tung*, 37.

[17]Edward L. Katzenbach, "The Revolutionary Strategy of Mao Tse-Tung," *Political Science Quarterly* 70, no. 3 (September 1955): 321-340, http://www.jstor.org/stable/2145469 (accessed September 2, 2010).

between 1920 to 1976.[18] This collection of work provided Mao's philosophies and

opinions on world events, the central government, and interactions with leadership. The

important works fell under three categories. The first category was Mao's ―Report on an

Investigation of the Peasant Movement In Hunan." In this investigation, Mao discussed

the abilities and effectiveness of a nearby peasant organization. Mao came to the

realization that a lower class population could organize within themselves.[19] A peasant

organization could form a formidable opponent against merchants and gentry taking

advantage of them. The second category of essays were ―On Contradiction," ―On

Practice," and ―Dialectical Materialism." These three essays discussed his views of

human nature and the justifications to form a single class of people to set the conditions

for China to progress. The third category consisted of those works that characterized

Mao's use of guerrilla warfare. These essays included ―On Protracted War" and

―Problems of Strategy in Guerrilla War Against Japan."

    ―Report On An Investigation of the Peasant Movement In Hunan" was one of

Mao's earliest works. In it, Mao defended and praised the rise of peasant associations in

Hunan. The realization of peasant effectiveness convinced him that this rural group could

act as the vanguard of revolutionary movements.[20] Mao observed how successful

---

[18]The Marxist Archive site, http://www.marxists.org/reference/archive/mao/selected-works/date-index.htm has a library of Mao Tse Tung's works in chronological order.

[19]Mao Tse Tung, ―Report On An Investigation of the Peasant Movement In Hunan," in *Selected Works of Mao Tse Tung* (Peking: Foreign Language Press, 1967), 1:27.

[20]Ibid., 1:32. ―This great mass of poor peasants, or altogether 70 percent of the rural population, are the backbone of the peasant associations, the vanguard in the overthrow of feudal forces"

organizations of peasant associations were able to leverage against evil gentry and tyrants. Mao's observations led him to believe that these associations had the potential to revise the existing Confucian system of authorities. These consisted of political, clan, religious, and masculine-centered establishments. To Mao, this antiquated system formed the basis of –imperialism, warlordism, and corrupt officialdom."[21] This system bound the Chinese people. In this groundbreaking investigation, Mao also examined the steps peasants used to mobilize successfully. Such steps comprised of implementing swift justice and restructuring administrative systems prone to corruption. Mao's study of mass mobilization could also be tied to the Taliban in order to understand the reasons for its success and the sources of angst that motivate groups to join revolutionary movements.

Three major works that formed the basis of his theories were –Dialectical Materialism," –On Practice," and –On Contradiction," and represented Mao's attempts to qualify as a Marxist practioner.[22] Mao wrote –On Contradiction" to describe the existence of contradictions in society. –On Practice" discussed the way people gained knowledge through experiences, and realizing where they fell in the grand scheme of society. Mao emphasized the need to take action if one was to learn or change their current social condition. –Dialectical Materialism" was Mao's description of the conflict between

---

[21]Ibid., 1:27. –The patriarchal-feudal class of local tyrants, evil gentry and lawless landlords is the cornerstone of imperialism, warlordism and corrupt officialdom."

[22]Stuart R. Schram, *Mao Tse Tung* (Baltimore: Penguin Books,1974), 223. Lecture notes on –Dialetical Materialism," –On Practice," and –On Contradiction" are part of a single effort by Mao to come to terms with the philosophical basis of Marxism. This led to the development of Maoism. See also Schram, *The Political Thought of Mao Tse-tung*, 87.

idealism and materialism, and the need to see the environment in terms of absoluteness or matter in order to accurately assess conditions of class and the state.

Mao wrote ―Dialectical Materialism‖ in 1938 as one of the foundational principles of Maoism. Mao in his lecture talked about how dialectical materialism was the thought process needed to rid society of classes, and enable it to progress. To Mao, the parochial system of Confucianism hindered the transformation of society.[23] By ridding the lines that separate economic classes, Mao hoped to bring the population to unite the classes and cause them to work together mutually. The lecture separated society in the categories of the oppressing and the oppressed. Mao stated that the oppressing classes were for the most part more idealist than they were materialist.[24] The oppressed formed the opposite category where they were more materialist than idealist.

The concept of idealism and materialism described two different methods used to interpret one‗s surroundings and gain situational understanding. Those who thought in a materialistic sense, generally interpreted his surroundings absolutely. This absolute is represented by matter. Matter is tangible and defined reality. According to Mao, idealism failed to take into account the real forms and descriptions of matter. These two schools of thought distinguished the various classes. In order to form one social system, this

---

[23]Mao Tse Tung, ―Dialectical Materialism,‖ in *The Political Thought of Mao Tse Tung* (New York: Praeger, 1970), 186. This book contains Mao‗s essay *Dialectical Materialism.* ―then we must struggle with all the old and rotten philosophical theories existing in China on the ideological front throughout the whole country.‖

[24]Ibid.,185. ―Idealism, in the process of its historical development, represents the ideology of the exploiting classes and serves reactionary purposes. Materialism, on the other hand, is the world view of the revolutionary class‖

boundary needed to disappear. Two steps were needed to eliminate the boundary between idealistic and materialistic thinking.

The first step required the oppressed class to see their position in society. The oppressed class had a tendency of looking at the world from a materialist perspective. It was up to the oppressed class to identify and enlighten the rest of society who saw their surroundings idealistically. This was the first step required to form a single class of society. This was the only way Mao believed the Chinese people could become a progressive society rather than cycle continuously through an ineffective system of hierarchical rule.

Society was the highest form of matter, and had its own true dynamic. Only a specific action could enlighten those in society who saw surroundings idealistically. Dialectical materialism was the specific method used to form a single class of society. Mao stated that each form of matter had a true movement or dynamic. Conditions for progression were reached once society removed idealism and one class was formed.

In ―On Contradiction," Mao made the case that everything in nature was made up of two parts that contradict.[25] These contradictions were also present in social orders. Contradictions could also be described as opposites. These opposites were inseparable and complemented one another. This interaction between the two kept them linked and formed a single identity. With this idea, one was capable of identifying contradictions within the social order. One example of this was the relationship between the proletariat and the bourgeoisie. One characteristic of the contradiction was that one side could

---

[25]Mao, ―On Contradiction," 1:317. For instance in mathematics integral and differential are contradictions. In physics positive and negative are contradictions.

transform into the other. For example, the worker and the supervisor were contradictions, but it was possible for the worker to become the supervisor.[26]

A second characteristic was that there existed a level of particularity when contradictions were coupled together. A correct linkage had to be made between the two. For instance, Mao stated colonies were contradictions to imperialism.[27] With each particular set of contradictions came a specific action that could resolve the difference between them. Mao claimed that the contradiction between the proletariat and the bourgeoisie was resolved by the method of socialist revolution.[28]

In the essay, "On Practice," Mao described his philosophies on the relationship between knowing and doing. It worked in conjunction with "On Contradiction" by the emphasis of three ideas. First, theorizing was useless without the chance to apply the theory. Second, only through application, could one gain further knowledge to refine approaches and reach desired endstates. Third, this knowledge enabled a man to apply actions that were accordant with the laws of the external world.[29]

---

[26]Ibid., 1:335. "In the revolutionary base areas under Communist leadership, the peasants have been transformed from being the ruled to being the rulers, while the landlords have undergone a reverse transformation."

[27]Ibid., 1:331. "The other contradictions such as those between imperialism and the colonies are all determined or influenced by this principle contradiction."

[28]Ibid., 1:321. "The contradiction between the proletariat and the bourgeoisie is resolved by the method of socialist revolution."

[29]Mao Tse Tung, "On Practice," in *Selected Works of Mao Tse Tung* (Peking: Foreign Languages Press,1967), 1:296.

First, Mao stated if someone sought knowledge, he must take part in the practice of changing reality and that all knowledge originated from direct experience.[30] The contradiction between the proletariat and the bourgeoisie was resolved through a social revolution. Knowledge used to conduct an effective revolution could not be gained without an attempt to determine its viability.

Second, one gained further knowledge and succeeded through continual application. Mao stated that after a person failed, he drew lessons, corrected his ideas, and made them correspond to the laws of the external world. Completing the preceding actions turned failure into success.[31] A purpose of the essay is to convince others that Maoism is a guide to action. Even though the revolution may occasionally fail, it is necessary to reach the ultimate end.

Third, this knowledge gave people a more holistic view of where they fell within the society. Mao stated that as man expanded his knowledge, he would eventually see his relationship with his fellow man in terms of material, political, and cultural life.[32] Once this realization occurred, man could act through revolution to resolve the contradictions that made up his identity.

One way Mao demonstrated practice was through his participation in guerrilla warfare. Mao outlined the function and role of guerrilla operations in ―On Protracted War" and ―Problems of Strategy in Guerrilla War against Japan." He recorded gained

---

[30]Ibid., 1:300. ―All genuine knowledge originates in direct experience."

[31]Ibid., 1:297. ―After he fails, he draws lessons, corrects his ideas to make them correspond to the laws of the external world, and can thus turn failure into success."

[32]Ibid., 1:296.

knowledge through these operations. Mao's ‑On Protracted War" described his overall

strategy to fight against the Imperial Japanese using guerrilla tactics. This strategy

consisted of three stages. The first covered a period of Mao's strategic defensive. The

second stage was the enemy's consolidation and preparation for counter-offensive. The

third was a counter-offensive followed by the enemy retreat.[33] The intent of Mao's

protracted war was to gain strategic victory through guerrilla tactics. It also included

exhausting the enemy and waiting for them to concede before moving on to a

conventional attack phase.

‑Problems of Strategy in Guerrilla War Against Japan" went through the

important elements guerrilla movements depended on preserving one's own strength and

destroying that of the enemy.[34] Guerrilla warfare incorporated the concepts of

contradiction and practice. The contradiction was between sacrifice and self-preservation.

The whole intent of guerrilla warfare revolved around preservation. Mao believed that in

order to achieve this, a guerrilla army must exploit the shortage of the enemy's troops and

maintain the notion the enemy was pursuing a barbarous policy.[35] One important aspect

of the research looked into Mao's emphasis on centralized command. To Mao, ‑guerrilla

warfare could not be successfully developed without some strategic centralized

---

[33]Mao Tse Tung, ‑On Protracted War," in *Selected Works of Mao Tse Tung* (Peking: Foreign Language Press, 1967), 2:140.

[34]Mao Tse Tung, ‑Problems of Strategy In Guerrilla War Against Japan," in *Selected Works of Mao Tse Tung* (Peking: Foreign Language Press, 1967), 2:81. ‑All guiding principles of military operations grow out of the one basic principle: to strive to the utmost to preserve one's own strength and destroy that of the enemy."

[35]Ibid., 2:86.

command."[36] This centralized command idea was vital in coordinating guerrilla warfare within the war zone, and may help provide insights on vulnerabilities within the Taliban regime.

References

Three references were indispensable to understand the Chinese Civil War and its important events. The first was Thomas Griess' *The Arab-Israeli Wars, the Chinese Civil War and the Korean War*. The section on the Chinese Civil War provided a detailed summary of the entire civil war. It provided explanations to why Sun Yat-sen, Mao and Chiang Kai Shek rose to power, and the impacts the Japanese invasion had on Mao's philosophies on imperialism and mass mobilization. The second important work was David A. Graff and Robin Higham's *A Military History of China*. These authors gave summaries of other internal disputes that occurred prior to the 1911 Chinese Civil War. It helped understand what China went through prior to Mao discovering Marxist-Leninism. The final reference was the Marxist Internet Archive.[37] This online source contained a library of all the works of the well known contemporary Marxists. Selected works from both Mao Tse Tung and Lenin were referenced from this site.

Scholars of Maoism

Stuart R. Schram provided two very important sources towards understanding the context and the evolution of Maoism. Schram wrote *The Political Thought of Mao Tse*

---

[36]Ibid., 2:110.

[37]Marxist Internet Archive. ―Selected Works of Mao Tse Tung," http://www.marxists.org/reference/archive/mao/index.htm (accessed March 29, 2011).

Tung and *Mao Tse Tung*. These two works were fundamental in gaining deeper understanding Mao's insights, his motivations toward starting his Chinese Communist revolution, and his use of Communist doctrine to reach his strategic end.

The Political Thought of Mao Tse Tung was a study in the writings of Mao within a span of fifty years from the pre-Marxist period to 1967. Schram worked in conjunction with other Chinese experts to trace the evolution of Mao's thought strictly through his major works. From the assessment, Schram evaluated Mao's role as a leader, originality of thought, and his departure from traditional Marxism-Leninism. Schram labeled Mao a revolutionary nationalist who used Marxism-Leninism to achieve modernization in his backward country under an authoritarian context.[38] Schram stated Maoism was unique in that Mao used the rural areas of China to stimulate and sustain his movement rather than industrial centers.[39] This work was important for the research because it suggested that revolutionary movements adapted to their circumstances and cultural environments.

Mao Tse Tung was a biography written by Schram. The first three chapters of this book were the most useful. These chapters described Mao's early childhood in Hunan, his days as a student in Changsha, and his exposure to Communism. Schram explained how the beginnings of the Chinese Revolution in 1911 and the period of warlordism shaped Mao's worldview. The volatility of the period led Mao into experimenting with various educational opportunities. At one point, he even joined Sun Yat-sen's army to help finish the revolution.[40]

---

[38]Schram, *Political Thought of Mao Tse Tung*, 133.

[39]Ibid., 137.

[40]Schram, *Mao Tse Tung*, 34.

18

Mao's wandering eventually led him to attend a school in Changsha where he intended to become a teacher. During Mao's education, instructors exposed him to their ideas on nationalism, explanations of China's current condition, and Communism.[41] Schram explained in *Mao Tse Tung* how the political vacuum shaped Mao's political thought and decisions.

Another biographical reference is Edgar Snow's *Red Star of China*. Snow wrote this book during the Japanese invasion of China. Snow provided insights on the effects of imperialism on Chinese national unity. The invasion caused an outpouring of support to the partisan movement. Snow depicted Mao as an insightful political reformer that was keenly aware of the endurance required to survive an insurgency against the Imperialist Japanese. Snow described how Mao engineered a political reform and propaganda machine to gain more popularity that resulted in the recruitment of the largest guerrilla force in the world. Mao's ability to portray Communist image as incorruptible contributed to getting massive support. Similarly, the Taliban gained early popularity by crafting an image that was pious and committed to restoring justice in the region. Snow also presented the importance of mass mobilization in guerrilla operations. This triggered the need to research mass mobilization deeper. To Mao, mass organizations were the guerrilla's sinew of life.[42] This suggested that other guerrilla organizations like the Taliban also saw mobilization as a key to its future success.

---

[41]Ibid., 48. At Peking University, Mao was exposed to Communism by the head of the Peking Library Li Ta-Chao and a professor named Yang Chang-chi on July 1918.

[42]Edgar Snow, *Red Star Over China* (New York: Grove Press, 1968), 451.

Phyllis Frakt's ―Mao's Concept of Representation" provided insights on the importance of mass mobilization in revolutionary movements.[43] Revolutionary leaders such as Mao and Lenin had to determine where popular support came from, and how the support would be controlled and maintained.[44] Another idea brought up by both of these authors was that a procedure needed to be put in place to respond immediately to the true concerns of the population. In Mao's case this was the mass-line theory.[45] Populist tactics were essential in maintaining the life of a revolution. If the selected demographic group was too small, it would in essence limit the effectiveness of the movement. If too large, the revolution would require more and faster means to meet the demands of the populist powerbase.

Maurice Meisner's journal articles and book delved into the relationship between Marxism, Leninism, and Maoism. ―Leninism and Maoism: Some Populist Perspectives on Marxism-Leninism in China" and ―The Maoist Legacy and the Chinese Socialism"

---

[43]Phyllis M. Frakt, ―Mao's Concept of Representation," *American Journal of Political Science* 23, no. 4 (November 1979), http://www.jstor.org/stable/2110802 (accessed October 15, 2010).

[44]Maurice Meisner, ―Leninism and Maoism: Some Populist Perspectives on Marxism-Leninism in China," *The China Quarterly*, 45 (January-March 1970): 26. Lenin had a problem of bridging the gap between the intelligentsia and the masses centres on the question of who are the bearers of true socialist consciousness and how that consciousness is to be fashioned into a historically dynamic revolutionary force. Meisner pg 10. Mao emphasized (at least until recent years) the indispensable leadership role of the Party, but he has also argued passionately that true revolutionary knowledge ultimately comes from the people themselves and that Party leaders and cadres must therefore ―learn from the masses " and " acquire the good qualities of workers and peasants."

[45]Frakt, ―Mao's Concept of Representation," 691.

both detailed the differences among the related ideologies.[46] He detailed Mao as not falling in line with hardcore Leninists, but implied that although the spirit of Communism existed within Mao, there were large differences on what intended group was in charge of the world revolution, as well as the development phases of nation-states when Communism was implemented in a European nation compared to an Asian one.[47]

Meisner also has a book entitled *Mao's China*. Meisner was a key reference to understand the differences of Maoism and knowing its lessons learned in social reform. It was also a history that centered on the development and modification of Communism. Meisner traced the evolution of the Communist ideology, the implementation of Mao's ideas on land reform, industrialization, land collectivization. Meisner stated in his work that Maoism in of itself was a unique derivative of classic Communism.

<u>Taliban Sources</u>

In order to better understand Taliban strategy, it is important to know the context behind the Taliban movement and methods the organization used to gain power. The author used several sources to understand the Taliban's history prior to the 9/11 attacks. These consisted of *The Taliban and the Crisis of Afghanistan, Taliban:Militant Islam, Oil and Fundamentalism in Central Asia, The Rise of the Taliban,* and *Koran, Kalashnikov*

---

[46]Meisner, ―Leninism and Maoism"; Maurice Meisner, ―The Maoist Legacy and Chinese Socialism," *Asian Survey* 17, no. 11 (November 1977): 1016-1027, http://www.jstor.org/stable/2643350 (accessed April 5, 2011).

[47]Maurice Meisner, *Mao's China* (London:Collier Macmillan Publishers, 1977), 49.

and Laptop.[48] These authors provided the history of the Taliban, and had entire chapters

explaining Taliban strategy and goals.

   The Taliban and the Crisis of Afghanistan discussed the Taliban's rise to power in

the early 1990s. Crews and Tarzi explained a macro-view of the Taliban, and thoroughly

discussed its inextricable link with Pakistan. The book was a diplomatic historical

reference and a political criticism on the inner-workings of the Taliban as a revolutionary

movement. Various authors in the book examined the Taliban's movement's political,

military and diplomatic elements to determine the causes behind its sudden rise,

propensity in moving through the convoluted world of Pastunwalli warlord politics, and

its focus on sharia law as an end all be all in administratively running state functions.

   Crews and Tarzi noted some of the flaws in the Taliban's revolutionary strategy.

One potential flaw and vulnerability was its rigid focus on the military aspect of its

movement with no regard to forming modern federal institutions. The Taliban would

eventually lose its power and credibility since its campaign plan is absent of any

economic and social reform.[49] Furthermore, the Inter-Service Intelligence (ISI) based its

---

[48]Robert D. Crews and Amin Tarzi, eds., *The Taliban and the Crisis of Afghanistan* (Cambridge: Harvard University Press, 2008); Neamatollah Nojumi, *The Rise of the Taliban in Afghanistan: Mass Mobilization, Civil War, and the Future of the Region* (New York: Palgrave, 2002); Ahmed Rashid, *Taliban: Militant Islam, Oil and Fundamentalism in Central Asia* (New Haven: Yale University Press, 2010); Antonio Guistozzi, *Koran, Kalashnikov, and Laptop: The Neo-Taliban Insurgency in Afghanistan* (New York: Columbia University Press, 2008).

[49]Neamatollah Nojumi, ―The Rise and Fall of the Taliban,‖ in *The Taliban and the Crisis of Afghanistan*, ed. Robert D. Crews and Amin Tarzi (Cambridge: Harvard University Press, 2008), 109. There are significant differences between a popular movement in opposition and one facing the challenges of governing once in power. Like many other revolutionary movements, the Taliban failed to differentiate between running a popular militaristic movement and administering a functioning state.

relationship with the Taliban's ability to gain and maintain control of Afghanistan. Part of the Taliban's survival, funding, and training depended on maintaining that relationship with the ISI. A break in this relationship led the ISI to seek a more effective group to accomplish Pakistan's strategic ends in the region. An example of this was when the ISI broke its relationship with Hikmatyar in favor of the burgeoning Taliban.[50] Crews and Tarzi delved into the populist dimension of the Taliban's success. This was attributed to the Taliban's keen understanding of Pashtun culture. The Taliban's understanding of Pashtun culture allowed them to leverage and use proper coercion techniques to force unity among tribes from Spin Boldak to Mazar-e-Sharif.[51]

Taliban by Ahmed Rashid provided a wealth of information on the Taliban following the withdrawal of Soviet forces in 1987. Rashid was another authoritative source for anyone studying the Taliban, its agenda, and strategic impacts. Rashid is a correspondent to Central Asia, Afghanistan and Pakistan for the *Far Eastern Economic Review*. The book was a culmination of his twenty-one years of experience in Afghan affairs.[52]

---

[50]Adulkader Sinno, ―Explaining the Taliban's Ability to Mobilize the Pashtuns," in *The Taliban and the Crisis of Afghanistan*, ed. Robert D. Crews and Amin Tarzi (Cambridge: Harvard University Press, 2008), 64. Nasirullah Khan Babar, Pakistan's interior minister was the chief advocate of shifting support from Hekmatyar to the Taliban.

[51]Sinno, ―Eplaining the Taliban's Ability to Mobilize the Pashtuns," 61. The Taliban were able to assimilate Pashtun leaders by making effective use of expert knowledge of the Pashtun power tapestry and devising sophisticated strategies that sidelined opposition at little cost.

[52]Amr Sabet, ―Reiew: Untitled," *British Journal of Middle Eastern Studies* 30, no. 1 (2003): 93. http://www.jstor.org.lumen.cgsccarl.com/stable/pdfplus/ 3593252.pdf?acceptTC=true (accessed April 5, 2011).

Rashid described how the Taliban movement evolved from Deobandi Islam into a unique and errant form of Islam as a result of the ideological vacuum from the post-Soviet invasion. The forming of extremist madrassas preached a version of Islam absent of context and Afghani history. As a result, students of these schools transformed into radical disciples, and trained to deem Taliban theology as inerrant.

Rashid, like Crews, also emphasized the Taliban's links to Pakistan's ISI, and described ISI's inability to gain dominance over the Taliban's affairs despite its ongoing assistance. Rashid described an organization that looked to the ISI to gain the capacity to capture Kabul in its initial stages, but went rogue eventually to pursue an ill-designed strategy to establish governance through a brutal interpretation of sharia law.[53] Rashid went on to explain how their application of sharia law erased any remnants of Afghanistan's culture and administrative capacity. These edicts issued by the Taliban relinquished the influence of women from their society, and removed traditions that took centuries to develop.[54]

Rashid depicted a bleak future for Afghanistan, and concluded that the Taliban was on the verge of splintering.[55] Taliban came as a result of a failed state that underwent years of civil war so chaotic that any group that could bring a sense of order would gain support from the population regardless of its ideology. Enabling the Taliban to impose

---

[53]Rashid, *Taliban:Militant Islam,Oil and Fundamentalism in Central Asia*, 185. Despite efforts to help and control the Taliban, they were nobody's puppets and they resisted every attempt by Islamabad to pull their strings.

[54]Ibid., 108. One fourth of the administration workforce was women, elementary teachers were women

[55]Ibid., 212. ―Divisions within the Taliban are multiplying so fast and it is not unlikely that more moderate Taliban may mount a coup against Mullah Omar and the Kandahari ulema."

sharia law caused a bad situation to become even worse. The skewed strategic priorities resulted in the disintegration of any remnant institutions and stopped support from the United Nations, and non-governmental organizations that had kept the country afloat.

The most recent book out of the four was *Koran, Kalishnikov, and Laptop: The Neo-Taliban Insurgency in Afghanistan* by Antonio Guistozzi.[56] Guistozzi departed from the others in that he went over the more recent strategies of the Taliban after being removed from power in 2001.[57] Guitozzi described the Taliban as an adaptive organization with a strategy that was changing constantly from lessons learned. Guitozzi mentioned the Taliban's current strategy was different from classic insurgencies of the 1940-1980s.[58] He assessed the Taliban has the ability to transform into an international movement one, rather than confined only in Afghanistan.

Many Taliban sources could be found in several online databases. These consist of Jane's Terrorism and Security Monitor and the Columbia International Affairs Online. Jane's Terrorism site contained the most recent Taliban events from the tactical to strategic levels. Columbia International Affairs Online had articles from major think tanks on the Taliban strategy like the American Enterprise Institute for Public Policy Research and the Carnegie Endowment for International Peace. A highly useful source

---

[56] Antonio Guistozzi, *Koran, Kalashnikov, and Laptop: The Neo-Taliban Insurgency in Afghanistan* (New York: Columbia University Press, 2008).

[57] Rashid, *Taliban:Militant Islam,Oil and Fundamentalism in Central Asia*, 266. On November 26, 2001, US Troops and Northern Alliance topple Mazar-e-Sharif, Heart, and Kabul.

[58] Guistozzi, *Koran, Kalashnikov and Laptop*, 234.

for researching Taliban strategy came from the *Petersberg Papers.*[59] This 198 page

volume was a compilation of speeches from various Afghan officials and experts. The

speeches detailed the obstacles the current government was facing against the Taliban.

These papers gave important insights on the effectiveness of the Taliban strategy from

the viewpoint of the Afghanistan central government.

Two research papers referenced several times in support of this research were *The

Evolution of the Taliban* by Shahid A. Afsar and Christopher A. Samples and *Human

Geography in Afghanistan-Pakistan-Region:Undermining the Taliban Using Traditional

Pashtun Social Structures.* These two research papers from the Naval Postgraduate

School (NPS) provided other references in support of the research. They also contained

answers on questions pertaining to the Taliban's strategy and emphasis on mass

mobilization.

The National Security Archive published a *September 11th Sourcebook* with

declassified US Embassy cables dealing with the Taliban.[60] This source provided first-

hand accounts of Taliban actions during their rise to power between 1996 and 2001. The

sourcebook was broken into three separate volumes. These volumes covered the

formation of the Taliban from the perspective of the US Embassy in Islamabad, Pakistan.

---

[59] Wolfgang Danspeckgruber. *Petersberg Papers on Afghanistan and the Region.* Vol. 4 of *Liechenstein Colloquium Report.* Princeton, NJ: Princeton University, 2009. http://www.ciaonet.org.lumen.cgsccarl.com/wps/lisd/0018577/f_0018577_15903.pdf (accessed September 2, 2010). Petersberg Papers is a result of a conference held by the Liechtenstein Institute on Self-Determination at Princeton University (LISD). In September 2008, the organization invited high-level governmental officials, experts, and other representatives to discuss important issues for Afghanistan in the region

[60] The National Security Archive, "The September 11th Sourcebooks," http://www.gwu.edu/~nsarchiv/NSAEBB/sept11 (accessed September 15, 2010).

As a whole, these documents formed a Pakistan-centric view of the Taliban. The collection emphasized that the Taliban's movement and the ISI are inextricably linked with one another.

The Nine Eleven Finding Answers Foundation online source provided a collection of messages from various terrorist leaders to include Mullah Omar.[61] These messages displayed the speed and effectiveness of the Taliban's informational campaign. The site also included video interviews with top Taliban leadership.

Another online source used was Peter Bergen's official webpage.[62] Bergen is a print and television journalist. He has reported on Afghanistan and Pakistan for several American newspapers and magazines. The articles dated from 1998 to the present. His articles provided supporting evidence that were useful in the research.

In terms of visual sources, National Geographic has a documentary entitled *Inside the Taliban*.[63] This visual resource summarized major events and showed who the key players were in the Taliban regime. Frontline also has several films that document first-hand accounts of Taliban operations and strategies. One of these films was entitled

---

[61]Nine Eleven Finding Answers (NEFA) Foundation, ―Translations/Transcriptions of Documents from Terrorist Groups: Afghanistan,‖ http://nefafoundation.org/ index.cfm?pageID=54 (accessed April 5, 2011).

[62]Peter Bergen.com. http://www.peterbergen.com/index.aspx (accessed February 14, 2011).

[63]David Keane. *Inside the Taliban,* Directed by David Keane. National Geographic Channel, 2010.

Behind the Lines with the Taliban. This film was produced by an Afghan journalist who lived with an insurgent cell in Afghanistan.[64]

The film depicted the Taliban cells as small *ad hoc* units comprised of a conglomeration of males from different parts of Afghanistan. They were supplemented with funds as well as foreign fighters with expertise in bomb making. These fighters displayed little understanding of any grand Taliban strategy except to rid the country of occupiers in the name of Allah. Cultural clashes among foreign fighters existed within their organization. It was apparent the conditions were ripe for even more decentralization in the Taliban organization to form potentially rogue or splinter organizations in the future. This film showed the level of organization, education, and cohesiveness inside terrorist cells.

---

[64]Najibullah Quraishi. *Behind Taliban Lines*, Produced by Ken Dornstein. Clover Films, 2010, http://www.pbs.org/wgbh/pages/frontline/talibanlines/ (accessed October 22, 2010).

CHAPTER 3

RESEARCH DESIGN

This research was a comparative study of two revolutionary movements. The Maoist model was an example of a complete and successful revolutionary movement that possessed an ample amount of research sources. The *Selected Works of Mao Tse Tung* and authoritative Chinese historical sources provided information on fundamental elements in revolutionary strategy. Using Maoism as a baseline for comparison, the researcher sought to gain insights on weaknesses in the Taliban's strategy. It was assumed elements of universality existed when it came to conducting revolutionary movements. Therefore, if the Taliban did not include these Maoism methods after comparison, it suggested a possible weakness existed in the Taliban's approach to achieve its own strategic ends.

Research Methodology

The research topic examined the Taliban's strategy using the fundamentals of Mao. Insights on the Taliban's strategic vulnerabilities were gained using this approach. Both the Mao and Taliban revolutionary movements had contextual similarities. For example, both China and Afghanistan transformed into failed stated after the previously existing government dissolved. Civil war followed by a period of warlordism characterized the transitional phase between the time the Qing Dynasty collapsed, and the point Mao gained power with his CCP. Similarly, after the fall of the Peoples Democratic

Party of Afghanistan, Afghanistan experienced a devastating six year civil war.[65] China

and Afghanistan also encountered ideological and political vacuums. These particular

similarities allowed for easier analysis, since they contained parallel phases. Thus, the

first part of the research was to determine the degree of historical similarity between both

revolutionary movements.

After understanding the similarities, the analysis ascertained whether Mao and

Omar used their revolutionary movements to solve similar problems. This required a

study of the major events that molded both movements' philosophies within these

ideological and political vacuums. What were the Taliban's reasons toward adopting

extremist anti-Western Islam ideologies and implementing? Why did Mao embrace

Marxist-Leninism as the core of Maoism? Answering these questions defined the

problem both movements attempted to solve.

The author used the research to understand the major precepts of both Maoism

and the Taliban. This portion of the research was the first step toward finding

vulnerabilities. The intent was to compare the completeness of the Taliban's strategy to

solve Afghanistan's problems to Mao's approach in China. This required reading several

of Mao's selected works in the areas of mass mobilization, his ideological theories, and

his ideas behind guerrilla warfare and protracted war.

In order to find Taliban vulnerabilities, Mao's *Selected Works* were separated into

three categories. These categories were comprised of Mao's theories, his problems in

achieving and maintaining mass mobilization to gain control of China, and the issues

_____

[65]The Afghanistan Civil War occurred 1987-1992 after the fall of Najibullah's
regime.

Mao faced in his participation in protracted war. Then relevant Taliban actions were researched to indicate whether or not the Taliban coincidentally followed Maoist theory. If there was an inconsistency, further research assessed whether this suggested a potential flaw or vulnerability in the Taliban's revolutionary strategy under the argument that Mao's revolutionary strategy worked and was successful.

The research determined that a successful revolutionary movement like Mao's required effective mobilization of the masses in order to build military forces and provided a means to build political power. Mao's *Selected Works* and journal articles on the subject provided a list of vital elements that contributed to successful mass mobilization. Four specific elements taken from Maoism and journal articles were the use of anti-imperialist themes, the use of coercive violence, mass-line theory, and hero worship.

The researcher studied The Taliban's recent actions to assess whether these same elements designed to achieve successful mass mobilization existed. Recent Taliban actions from books, newspaper articles, recent journal articles, and online search engines provided information necessary to understand the Taliban's behavior. The Taliban's mobilization efforts were diagnosed off of a Maoist standard to determine whether possible vulnerabilities existed in the Taliban's approach to maintain effective cohesion.

The third area that was compared to gain insights on Taliban vulnerabilities was Mao's use of guerrilla warfare and his ideas on protracted war. Protracted war was a politically-charged method Mao used to fight against Japanese imperialism during the midpoint of the Chinese Civil War.[66] The research first presented the way Mao's

protracted war was organized using his works "On Protracted War" and "Problems with

Strategy in Guerrilla War Against Japan." This organization consisted of a strategic

defensive, preparation for counteroffensive, and the actual execution of the

counteroffensive.[67]

Research of recent events assessed whether the Taliban were following a similar

version of Mao's protracted war. From this comparison, the author suggested

vulnerabilities in Taliban strategy by first pinpointing what phase the Taliban were

currently operating in Mao's protracted war template. Knowing which phase in protracted

war allowed the author to determine whether the corresponding vulnerabilities Mao

expressed were applicable to the Taliban's situation.

---

[66]Stephen R. MacKinnon, "The Sino-Japanese Conflict 1931-1945," in *A Military History of China*, ed. David A. Graff and Robin Higham (Cambridge: Westview Press, 2002), 212.

[67]Mao, "On Protracted War," 2:136.

CHAPTER 4

ANALYZING AND INTERPRETING THE EVIDENCE

Maoism

In order to understand Maoism, it was important to grasp the principles of Marxist-Leninism. It was even more important to understand the intent of Marxist-Leninism as well. Lenin believed a society could evolve and transform into a utopian society based on a –common control of production in the interest of reciprocity, expressive work, and the satisfaction of the needs characteristic of cooperating human beings.”[68] To reach this point required following stages of Marx's revolutionary doctrine. The beginning stages involved an armed uprising of oppressed working class proletariat led by Communist Party leadership. The enemy was the oppressive capitalistic bourgeoisie.[69] After the armed uprising, the proletariat gained political control. The proletariat's gaining of political control led to an economic change where socialization occurred and private property was abolished.[70] Eventually, the whole concept of the state ceased to exist resulting in a stateless and classless society.[71]

Historical Context Behind Maoism

By 1911, China had already fought sixty years of war both internally and against foreign powers. Engagements such as the Opium Wars in 1856 against the British and

---

[68]Steven M. Cahn ed., *Classics of Political and Moral Philosophy*, 828.

[69]Roy C. Macridis, *Contemporary Political Ideologies* (Cambridge: Winthrop Publishers, 1980), 130.

[70]Ibid.

[71]Ibid.

33

Russo-Japanese War shaped China's negative perceptions of capitalist Western foreign powers.[72] Foreign powers France, Great Britain, and Russia had taken control of most of the major economic coastal centers, and forced the Chinese into unfair trading practices.[73] The Taiping Rebellion, Boxer Rebellion, and the Chinese Civil War taught the Chinese the powerful effects of outside ideas on the population as well as an understanding how these ideas could break China apart.[74]

The central government became more powerless. The credibility of the Manchu Dynasty decreased based on its inability to maintain stability. Eventually, Sun Yat-Sen's Republican Revolution would force the Manchu rulers to step down and be replaced by a provisional Republic of China.[75] China transitioned into a state of control under a league of warlords that brought order, and in some cases justice in their respective zones.

At the conclusion of World War I, the Treaty of Versailles officially ended the war. Through the treaty, allied leaders allowed Imperial Japan to seize German concessions in north China.[76] This action caused a wave of widespread nationalism and protest. In reaction, the Chinese looked for solutions to transform China into a strong and modern nation. Many Chinese such as Mao looked to Lenin's version of Communism to fulfill these goals.

---

[72]Edward L. Dreyer, ―Continuity and Change,‖ in *A Military History of China*, ed. David A. Graff and Robin Higham (Cambridge: Westview Press, 2002), 34.

[73]Thomas E. Greiss, ed., *The Arab Israeli Wars, The Chinese Civil War, and the Korean War* (Wayne, NJ: Avery Publishing, 1987), 34.

[74]Ibid.

[75]Snow, *Red Star Over China*, xx-xxi.

[76]Griess, *The Arab Israeli Wars, The Chinese Civil War, and the Korean War*, 37.

Sun Yat-sen integrated the Chinese Communists into his Nationalist effort in exchange for Lenin's military advisory support and equipment. Led by Chiang Kai Shek, the Nationalists and Communists managed to fight the warlords through the Northern Expedition and unite the country under the KMT.[77] After reunification, the KMT and the CCP debated over the next strategic step. By this point, the left-wing CCP organized peasant movements again threatening China's stability.[78] In reaction, Chiang Kai Shek exterminated several thousand communists. The massacre forced remaining communists to scatter into the rural areas.

The communists took advantage of this by organizing peasant associations, and mobilized the peasants successfully throughout south-central China in preparation to take control of the country. By 1930, the Chinese Civil War began between the KMT and the CCP. In 1937, the Imperial Japanese invaded China.[79] A temporary alliance between the KMT and CCP was formed to fight against the Japanese and brought the Civil War to a standstill. This alliance lasted until 1945 upon Japan's surrender after the bombing of Hiroshima, and the end of World War II.

These events shaped Mao's ideology. Mao encountered the damaging effects of the political vacuum. He also saw how a weak government could be swayed easily by corruption and exploitation by Western powers. During the Chinese Civil War, he also experienced the impact a united front had on bringing unprecedented cohesion among various political groups. Thus, from these past experiences, Mao saw that his ideology

---

[77]Griess, *The Arab Israeli Wars, The Chinese Civil War, and the Korean War*, 39.

[78]Ibid., 40.

[79]Ibid., 49.

needed to bring a majority of the population together to regain China's prominence, and resist against the actors that led to its previous downfall. Leninism provided the framework to develop his ideology.

The "Sinification" of Leninism

Leninism provided "a plausible, if incomplete explanation of history and ideal for social organization, and a detailed strategy for mobilizing, organizing and bringing these changes about."[80] Lenin did not believe that his ideology could apply to countries like China. Lenin referred to China as a "backward country."[81] These were the countries that did not have the industrial-based capacity to undergo a social transformation under classic Communist theory. Lenin believed that only the proletariat and the bourgeoisie had ability to affect society.[82] Traditional Leninism emphasized a need for organization. One major departure from Maoism was Lenin's use of gifted individuals that act on behalf of the proletariat. This group is referred to as a vanguard.[83] This portion of the

---

[80]Ibid.

[81]Karl A. Wittfogel,"The Marxist View of China (Part 2)," *The China Quarterly* no. 12 (1962): 154, http://www.jstor.org.lumen.cgsccarl.com/stable/651821?& Search=yes&searchText=2&searchText=View&searchText=Marxist&searchText=Part& searchText=China&list=hide&searchUri=%2Faction%2FdoBasicSearch%3FQuery%3D The%2BMarxist%2BView%2Bof%2BChina%2B%2528Part%2B2%2529%26acc%3Do n%26wc%3Don&prevSearch=&item=1&ttl=8894&returnArticleService=showFullText (accessed May 4, 2011).

[82]Mostafa Rejai, *Political Ideologies: A Comparative Approach* (Armonk: M.E. Sharpe, 1995), 53. "Peasants were below the proletariat and bourgeoisie and according to Leninism only those two classes were capable of establishing domination over society as a whole."

[83]Macridis, *Contemporary Political Ideologies*, 132.

Communist party steered the agenda of the proletariat with a clear understanding of the party's goals and the totality of society's interests.[84]

According to Lenin, peasants could be helpful in revolution, but incapable of actually running the revolution leading to socialism.[85] One reason was based off his presumption that the peasant had a natural desire to own their own land which went against the Marxist principles. By the Third International Congress in 1920, he upgraded the role for the peasant to act side by side with the proletariat, but Lenin was still distrustful of peasants.[86]

Mao in contrast believed that China's peasants had the ability to organize and run the revolution in entirety against oppressors. Mao justified this in his ―Report on An Investigation of Peasant Movement in Hunan."[87] Mao examined a particular uprising that had occurred in Hunan province between peasants and what he referred to as local tyrants and evil gentry.[88] In the report, Mao described various economic and populist tactics the peasants used to strike fear in the local tyrants and empower themselves. He referred to these methods as the ―Fourteen Great Achievements."[89]

The means to which the Hunan peasants built their powerbase came from the formation of peasant associations. Peasant associations in Hunan were well organized

---

[84]Ibid.

[85]Ibid.

[86]Rejai, *Political Ideologies: A Comparative Approach*, 172.

[87]Mao, ―Report On An Investigation of the Peasant Movement In Hunan," 1:24.

[88]Ibid., 1:25.

[89]Ibid., 1:34.

with membership numbers rising into the millions.[90] When organized, the peasants spoke

in mass against local tyrants, evil gentry, and corrupt officials. The peasantry possessed

the biggest potential powerbase for revolution. Peasant associations forced former

oppressors to comply with them in regards to wages and fair practices. The associations

also provided mutual protection amongst individual peasants.

Maoism was also distinctive from Leninism in its concepts of imperialism.

Lenin's definition of imperialism was an economic one.[91] To Lenin, imperialism was a

period of control by the big banks that had investments in oversea colonies, and the

division of the world into colonial areas areas of domination and exploitation.[92] Mao

focused anti-imperialist views specifically against Western countries. The British, French

and Russians forced the Chinese to sign a series of treaties that imposed heavy

indemnities, and allowed the westerners to administer large regions on behalf of the

Chinese Government. These acts of unfair economic practices fueled Mao's ideas of anti-

imperialism and Western hegemonism. Mao believed Western powers contributed to the

desecration of China, and helped bring the country to ruin. He also attributed the

weakening of China to specific classes of society that worked closely with imperialists.

To Mao, the classes that maintained imperialism were the ―warlords, bureaucrats, the

---

[90]Ibid. Mao states peasant associations in Hunan's 37/75 counties reached 1,367,727.

[91]Macridis, *Contemporary Political Ideologies*, 134.

[92]Ibid.

comprador class, the big landlord class, and the reactionary section of intelligentsia."[93] This set of classes embodied the parochial nature of Confucianism.[94]

Therefore, Mao attributed the ancient philosophies of Confucianism in hindering the country reaching full potential.[95] During the same period, an ideological vacuum occurred. The invasion of ideas such as democracy, liberty, individualism posed serious problems. Mao saw this phenomenon as a byproduct of imperialism. In addition, according to Mao the intrusion of various ideologies had already caused China internal chaos, and made it difficult to resolve contradictions among the masses.[96] Thus, Mao used anti-imperialism as a means to control the ideological vacuum. Mao also used these anti-imperialist views as a mechanism to create a powerful sense of nationalism throughout China.

Mao's use of peasants as a revolutionary force, focused on Western powers in his ideas of imperialism, and cultivated a third unique area of Maoism that departs from Leninism. This area is nationalism. While Leninism strived to do away with the state system altogether by reaching the utopian stage of Communism, Mao sought to do the opposite and strengthened the state. During the Chinese Civil War, Communists claimed

---

[93]Mao,"Analysis of the Classes in Chinese Society," in *Selected Works of Mao Tse Tung* (Peking: Foreign Languages Press, 1967), 1:13-22.

[94]Ibid., 1:13. —These classes represent the most backward and most reactionary relations of production in China and hinder the development of her productive forces. Their existence is utterly incompatible with the aims of the Chinese revolution."

[95]Mao Tse Tung,"Dialectical Materialism," in *The Political Thought of Mao Tse Tung*, 186. —Then we must struggle with all the old and rotten philosophical theories existing in China on the ideological front throughout the whole and liquidate the philosophical heritage of ancient China."

[96]Schram, *The Political Thought of Mao Tse Tung*, 312.

to be the only ―truly national force, fighting not only the Imperial Japanese but, the British and Americans as well."[97] Building nationalism helped Mao's Communists gain appeal.

Historical Context of the Taliban

The Taliban movement originated as a derivative of Deobandi Islam.[98] The formation of Deobandi Islam arose in British India as a movement to ―aform and unite Muslim society as it struggled to live within the confines of a colonial state."[99] In 1857, Indian Deobandis led an anti-British revolt, and were defeated.[100] Deobandis sought to revive and reinvent the modern Muslim as one that would ―revive Islamic values based on intellectual learning, spiritual experience, Shariah law and Tariqah or the path."[101] As a result, schools in support of Deobandi spread all across South Asia. These were referred to as madrassas.

In 1933, King Zahir Shah, the king of Afghanistan, worked with Deoband to set up state controlled madrassas. Eventually the madrassas expanded and transformed into the Jamiat-e-Ulema Islam religious movement whose purpose was to propogate their beliefs and mobilize the community of believers.[102] By 1988, there were 8,000 madrassas

---

[97]Macridis, Contemporary Political Ideologies, 174.

[98]Rashid, *Taliban:Militant Islam, Oil and Fundamentalism in Central Asia*, 88.

[99]Ibid.

[100]Ibid.

[101]Ibid.

[102]Ibid., 89.

with 25,000 unregistered ones, educating half a million students.[103] Pakistan's ISI played a large role in recruiting and funding madrassas especially during the era of Soviet expansion. These Deoband madrassas were aligned deliberately along the Pakistani border so that students could be indoctrinated quickly, and fight against the Soviet Union's invasion. Rivalry among madrassas organizations ensued based on competition for funding the ISI.

After the Soviet Union withdrew in 1988, the existing Peoples Democratic Republic of Afghanistan was left to fend for itself. In nearly ten years of Soviet occupation, the Red Army along with Afghan allies killed 1.3 million Afghans and completely destroyed the infrastructure in both the urban and rural areas.[104] By 1992 the Najibullah's regime ceased to exist.[105] Mujaheddin groups from both the north and the south raced to secure power in as large an area as possible. The power vacuum following the fall of Najibullah regime led to a destructive civil war amongst the Mujaheddin leadership and ravaged whatever was left in the country. Warlordism across Afghanistan was rampant. In 1994, President Burhanuddin Rabbani controlled the northeast portion of Afghanistan, and Kabul. Three provinces in the west centering on Herat were controlled

---

[103]Ibid.

[104]The Russian General Staff, *The Soviet-Afghan War:How a Superpower Fought and Lost*, ed. and trans. Lester W. Grau and Micheal A. Gress (Lawrance, KS: University Press of Kansas, 2002), 255-256.

[105]Martin Ewans, *Afghanistan: A Short History of Its People and Politics* (New York: HarperCollins, 2002), 178.

by Ismael Khan. Mujaheddin based in Jalalabad controlled the eastern area along the Pakistan border. The south and east of Kabul was controlled by Gulbuddin Hikmetyar.[106]

In 1993, the ISI looked for new ways to install a Pakistan-friendly central government within Afghanistan. The Deoband and its Jamiat-e-Ulema Islam had built strong relations with Pakistan's Bhutto Regime and the head of ISI, General Naseerullah Babar. Babar searched for a Pashtun group that could provide safe and controlled access through Afghanistan to benefit Pakistan's trade around Central Asia.[107]

Major roads throughout Afghanistan allowed goods to be shipped efficiently through Helmand province and Central Asia. Yet volatility from ongoing civil war resulted in a continual lack of situational control. Many of Pakistan's cargo transport trucks had to go through several improvised checkpoints. Warlord factions had seized portions of the major roads and demanded payment so that cargo drivers could get through. It was here that the Taliban grabbed the attention of the Pakistan's ISI. The ISI invested much to help Hikmetyar gain control of all Kabul, but was ineffective in taking full control of the city.[108] The ISI looked to find a better organization that could set the conditions to institute a Pakistan-friendly regime that could enhance its trade economy.

The Jamiat-e-Ulema Islam offered to take on this mission based on its strong relationship with Prime Minister Benazir Bhutto's regime. Deobandi tradition in the

---

[106]Rashid, *Taliban:Militant Islam, Oil and Fundamentalism in Central Asia*, 21.

[107]Ibid., 90.

[108]Ibid., 188. ―When the Taliban emerged the ISI was initially skeptical about their chances. It was a period when ISI was in retreat, with the failure of Hikmetyar to capture Kabul and a shortage of funds. The ISI retreat gave the Bhutto government the opportunity to devise their own support for the Taliban."

Jamiat-e-Ulema Islam had split since there was no existing central hierarchy in its network of madrassas. One of these split groups formed the core of what is now known as the Taliban. The ISI chose to hire the Taliban to provide security to protect Pakistan's supply convoys.[109] The Taliban first took control of Spin Boldak, an important city and entrance point between Pakistan and Afghanistan.[110] This required seizing the city from Hekmetyar as well. Once the Taliban proved it could take over Spin Boldak and the major roads within Afghanistan, it provided Pakistan escort capability to ship materials through Afghanistan securely.

The Taliban also embodied a successful, but brutal way to restore justice and order in the country. A series of events allegedly triggered the formation of the Taliban. During the spring of 1994, a local warlord in Kandahar had kidnapped madrassa students and proceeded to abuse them in his compound.[111] In reaction, Mullah Omar, the soon to be leader of the Taliban gathered students from local madrassas, rescued the victims, and killed the warlord.[112]

---

[109]Nojumi, *The Rise of the Taliban in Afghanistan:Mass Mobilization, Civil War, and the Future of the Region*, 118. In October 1994, the Taliban seized the military garrison in Kandahar and kept commercial roads secure and free for exports, imports and travelers.

[110]Rashid, *Taliban:Militant Islam, Oil and Fundamentalism in Central Asia*, 27.

[111]U.S. Embassy (Islamabad), Cable, ―Finally, A Talkative Talib: Origins and Membership of the Religious Students' Movement," February 20, 1995, Confidential, 6. http://www.gwu.edu/~nsarchiv/NSAEBB/NSAEBB97/tal8.pdf (accessed 23 October 2010).

[112]Ewans, *Afghanistan: A Short History of Its People and Politics,*182. Ewans states that this story on the Taliban inception reads well, but that the Taliban movement was formed more deliberately through funding and training from the ISI.

Such acts of justice brought immediate support and fame to the Taliban.[113] ISI

assessed the Taliban as the one group that could bring lasting security and order to the

ravaged country. A string of successes followed Spin Boldak. The Taliban seized the

capital city of Kabul on 5 November 1994.[114] The Taliban continued its campaign to take

control of all Afghanistan. In 1996, twenty-one of the thirty provinces were under

Taliban control.[115]

Northern Afghanistan was more difficult to seize. The population was not

Pashtun. Tajiks, Uzbeks, and Hazaras lived in the northern regions. At this point the

Taliban realized that organization was not one to share power, but planned to take over

all of Afghanistan. In addition, sharia law would be enforced immediately upon takeover

of the areas such as Mazar-e-Sharif which for the most part were untouched throughout

the Soviet invasion and following the Civil War. The Taliban managed to reach Bamiyan

a Tajik and Uzbek stronghold. The Taliban executed six thousand civilians as an act of

reprisal in addition to a hasty attempt to push out Shia influence from Northern

Afghanistan.[116] By 1997, the Taliban had taken over most of Afghanistan.

Forceful mobilization of the Pashtun population, and funding from the ISI led to

its streak of success. This made Mullah Omar a revered symbolic figure of the Taliban.

He had accomplished something that no other Afghan could. He had formed a fragile

conglomerate of tribes from Helmand to Kabul. He along with his followers seized the

---

[113]Rashid, *Taliban:Militant Islam, Oil and Fundamentalism in Central Asia*, 24.

[114]Ibid., 256.

[115]Ibid., 54.

[116]Ibid., 74.

44

capital. In addition, as a symbol of his mandate from Allah to reform the country, Mullah Omar decided to symbolize his mission and role by wearing a garment that once belonged allegedly to the Prophet Mohammed himself.[117]

The Taliban imposed harsh sharia which included continued massive atrocities against the non-Sunni population. Mullah Omar interacted with Osama bin Laden and hosted training camps and provided leadership in areas under their control. After the 11 September 2001 attacks on the United States, the Taliban refused to hand over the Al-Qaeda leaders responsible for orchestrating them. The Taliban considered forcing Osama Bin Laden out of the country of Afghanistan, but Taliban leader Mullah Omar was committed not to turn against him.[118] The United States led an invasion and ousted the Taliban from power. The Taliban fled Afghanistan following the attacks, and are currently operating along the Pakistan-Afghanistan border.[119]

---

[117]Ibid., 42. On April 4, 1996, Omar appeared on the roof of a building in the center of the city, wrapped in the cloak of the Prophet Mohammed, which had been taken out of its shrine for the first time in 60 years.

[118]U.S. Embassy (Islamabad) Cable, ―Afghanistan: In July 2 Meeting, (Excised) Defends Discriminatory Edicts on Women and Girls, and Controls on NGO's," July 2, 1998, Confidential, 7. http://www.gwu.edu/~nsarchiv/NSAEBB/NSAEBB97/talib9.pdf (accessed October 22, 2010).

[119]Jane's World Insurgency and Terrorism, ―Taliban," http://www4.janes.com. lumen.cgsccarl.com/subscribe/jwit/doc_view.jsp?K2DocKey=/content1/janesdata/binder/ jwit/jwit0270.htm@current&Prod_Name=JWIT&QueryText=%3CAND%3E%28%3CO R%3E%28%28%5B80%5DTaliban+%3CIN%3E+body%29%2C+%28%5B100%5D+% 28%5B100%5DTaliban+%3CIN%3E+title%29+%3CAND%3E+%28%5B100%5DTalib an+%3CIN%3E+body%29%29%29%29 (accessed October 22, 2010).

Taliban Political Ideology

The Taliban sought to establish its IEA under the ideology of the *Khelafat*. The state was intended to run under Islamic law referred to as shariah.[120] The Taliban designated Mullah Omar the *amir ul-mumanin* (the leader of believers) when the Taliban seized Kabul on 4 April 1996.[121] As the leader of believers, Mullah Omar was bestowed the authority to rule Afghanistan under a system of sharia law. The implementation of shariah was discussed by a group of religious scholars referred to as a *khalifah*.[122] Regardless of the interpretation, the leader of believers was the ultimate decision making authority. Two bodies enforced sharia-based decisions. The religious police carried out what was decided in the Islamic courts and also conducted punishment.[123] In addition, the Taliban stood up a Department for Preservation of Virtue and Elimination of Vice to enforced the leader of the faithful's decrees. These decrees included the declaration of jihad whereby qualified Muslims were expected to fight.[124]

The ideology of the *Khelafat* aimed at —ding mischief, establish peace and security, protect life, wealth and honor, enforce sharia, and make the land of Afghanistan an exemplary state. Yet in terms of economic reform, the Taliban had virtually no plan.[125]

---

[120]Nojumi, *The Rise of the Taliban in Afghanistan:Mass Mobilization, Civil War, and the Future of the Region*, 152.

[121]Rashid, *Taliban:Militant Islam, Oil and Fundamentalism in Central Asia*, 42.

[122]Nojumi, *The Rise of the Taliban in Afghanistan:Mass Mobilization, Civil War, and the Future of the Region*, 152.

[123]Ibid., 154.

[124]Ibid.

[125]Ibid., 175.

This was attributed to the absence of skilled professionals in the country. Without skilled professionals, there was no ability to gain professional knowledge that supported nation-building.[126]

Taliban Strategy

There were two periods that needed to be analyzed for the research. These two periods included the strategic actions used by the Taliban before and after 9/11. Before 9/11, the Taliban's strategy aimed at establishing a functioning IEA. Achieving this required the application of sharia law in all aspects of society. These laws did not allow meaningful development of governmental institutions such as health and education infrastructure. Sharia disallowed and marginalized the utilization of much of the remaining intellectual capital from providing their services to the general population.[127] As a result, the Taliban relied mostly on nongovernmental organizations and humanitarian aid organizations to replace the IEA's nonexistent governmental services. Understanding the nation-building strategy prior to 9/11 provided a glimpse of what the Taliban would do if the organization regained control of Afghanistan.

Antonio Guistozzi provided an overview of Taliban strategy after 9/11 in *Koran, Kalishnikov, and Laptop: The Neo-Taliban Insurgency in Afghanistan*.[128] The post

---

[126]Ibid., 176.

[127]Rashid, *Taliban:Militant Islam, Oil and Fundamentalism in Central Asia,* 125. ―There is no educated or professional class left in the country. In the several waves of refugees that left the cities since 1992, all the educated, trained professionals, even telephone operators, electricians, and mechanics have gone."

[128]Guistozzi, *Koran, Kalashnikov and Laptop: The Neo-Taliban Insurgency in Afghanistan.*

Taliban strategy was broken down into three distinct phases. These phases were the infiltration of the population, the creation of political structures, and the final offensive. The first phase required the Taliban to infiltrate the population. The Taliban entered various villages to identify facilities and people that were willing to provide sustenance, facilities, and spaces to hide weapons in support of insurgency operations.[129]

The development of political structures depended upon marginalizing the existing central government's efforts to rebuild institutions, and replacing them with a shadow government. Actions in support included assassination of intellectual capital required to maintain governmental services like teachers, doctors, and policemen.[130] This also included damaging important government facilities like schools.[131] Ruining the government's efforts to reestablish governmental services opened opportunities for the Taliban to substitute them with its own services.[132]

The final stage entailed a coordinated offensive. The Taliban attempted to conduct this third phase in 2006, but failed possibly from effective counterinsurgency operations prior.[133] Currently, it was believed that the Taliban continued to seek support from the Muslim community in terms of funding and manpower. If the Taliban succeeded in delegitimizing the central government, then the Taliban's next step would be to establish

---

[129]Ibid., 100.

[130]Ibid., 102.

[131]Ibid., 103. In 2006-2007, the Taliban attacked 187 schools.

[132]Ibid., 104.

[133]Ibid., 123.

firm control of eastern and southern Afghanistan, push to influence western Pakistan and reestablish its version of the Islamic state.[134]

Parallels in History

Understanding the parallels between both Mao's and Omar's rise helped gain insights in potential vulnerabilities in the Taliban's strategy. The similarities in events showed that each movement was left to solve a similar type of problem. There was also congruence in the type of actors and mechanisms used to implement each movement strategy. The analysis provided the basis and justification to use Maoism in this comparative study.

Historically, the movements fell under a similar set of events and circumstances. Several parallels existed between the rise of Mao's and Omar's respective movements. These similarities included the sort of causes and resulting general condition of the state prior to each movement's formation. Western power intervention in both countries was followed immediately by a collapse of the former regime. The collapse of the former regimes led to civil wars and a period of warlordism.

The Manchu dynasty lost its power in 1912.[135] Once the Qing dynasty collapsed, civil war ensued throughout the country. In the case of Afghanistan, collapse of the

---

[134]Shahid A. Asfar and Christopher A. Samples, "The Evolution of the Taliban," (Master's thesis, Naval Postgraduate School, 2008), 42, http://www.dtic.mil/srch/search?searchview=d4&c=t3&changequery=1&template=%2Fdtic%2Fsearch%2Ftr%2Fresults-template tr.html&s=1&fql=y&exact=n&xml=1&must1=and&pdfitems=&enable Lemmatization=YES&q=&field1=TI&word1=The+Evolution+of+the+Taliban&must2=AND&field2=AU&word2=&must3=AND&field3=KEY&word3=&must4=AND&field4=NU&word4=&must5=AND&field5=AB&word5=&must6=AND&field6=AB&word6=&must7=AND&field7=DE&word7=&must8=AND&field8=SC&word8=&Submit=Submit+Query&newold=date&age=any&sort=-RD&n=30 (accessed May 2, 2011).

49

Peoples Democratic Party of Afghanistan was followed by a five year civil war.[136] Civil

war caused both China and Afghanistan to spiral into chaos. This cycle of similar events

presented an opportunity for movements like the CCP and Taliban to gain control of the

country.

The respective civil wars set conditions for ideological vacuums. Throughout

China's Civil War from 1916 to 1922, the ideas of Communism, capitalism, nationalism,

socialism, and democracy each strived to take the place of the Confucian society.[137] In

Afghanistan's Civil War, ideas of extremist Islam, nationalism, and traditionalism

competed as the dominant philosophy. Both China and Afghanistan remained in a state of

flux or stalemate as a result of continued competition and disagreement over what

political ideology best suited overseeing a possible phase of reconstruction. In China the

stalemate period included a varying number of competing warlords who maneuvered

politically by using military force.[138] In Afghanistan the loose alliances between the

various Mujaheddin crumbled, and everyone started to pursue their own goals.[139] In

order to settle this ideological stalemate within each respective countries, both the CCP

---

[135]Greiss, *The Arab Israeli Wars, The Chinese Civil War, and the Korean War*, 33.

[136]Nojumi, *The Rise of the Taliban in Afghanistan:Mass Mobilization, Civil War, and the Future of the Region*, ii.

[137]Snow, *Red Star Over China*, xxiii.

[138]Greiss, *The Arab Israeli Wars, The Chinese Civil War, and the Korean War*, 36.

[139]Zaeef, *My Life With the Taliban*, 48.

and the Taliban needed to implement a revolutionary strategy to reconcile warlords and dominate internal competing ideologies.

Both movements worked with more powerful political elements. In Mao's case, it was the Communist Comintern which provided intellectual guidance and support for the CCP. For the Taliban the more powerful political element was the ISI. The Communist Comintern and the ISI both had strategic agendas separate from the individual movement. The Communist Comintern desired worldwide revolution. China on the other hand used Communist ideology to reinvent its central government, and reunite the country. The ISI wished to form a regime in Afghanistan that was Pakistan-friendly and stable.[140] The Taliban wished to establish an IEA.

Parallels in Political Ideology Intended Enstates

Although the means of each movement's strategy were very different, the general endstate for both the CCP and the Taliban were similar. In addition, the root causes for frustration that led to the development of the movements were also similar. Mao's and Omar's motivations to start their movements came from a desire to restore their respective countries into a state of former glory. Their targeted frustrations were based on the presence of corruption, and that these corrupt practices caused China and Afghanistan's current state of affairs.

Both countries experienced a period of invasion from outside powers and civil war. These countries suffered large losses in population and infrastructure as a result. Although Lenin wanted to rid the concept of the State, Mao's ideology aimed to restore

---

[140]Afsar, ―The Evolution of the Taliban," 37.

51

the strength of China. Schram believed that Mao's sense of nationalism led him to accept Leninism.[141] Mao stated that —the great union of the Chinese people must be achieved. Gentlemen! We must all exert ourselves, we must all advance with the utmost strength. Our golden age, our age of brilliance and splendor, lies ahead!"[142] This quotation expressed his belief that China could regain former glory.

Mullah Omar spoke of transforming Afghanistan into an —exemplary state of Islam."[143] Omar's aims and objectives comprised of regaining the status quo that existed prior to the US-led invasion in October 2001. Yet the desire of restoring the traditional Islamic system of the *Khelafat* demonstrated a desire by the Taliban to restore a system that represented an age when the Islamic state was at its height in scientific and military superiority.[144]

Targeted frustrations in both strategies were also similar. One of the basic functions of each ideology was to get rid of institutions of corruption. Each movement believed that corrupt practices contributed heavily to the downfall of their respective societies. Based on the historical context, Mao targeted Western powers and those Chinese elements of society that worked hand-in-hand with them. In *Analysis of the Classes in Chinese Society*, Mao believed that enemies of the revolutionary movement

---

[141]Mao Tse Tung,"To the Glory of the Hans," in *The Political Thought of Mao Tse Tung* (New York: Praeger, 1970), 161.

[142]Ibid., 164.

[143]Nojumi, *The Rise of the Taliban in Afghanistan:Mass Mobilization, Civil War, and the Future of the Region*, 154.

[144]Andrew Hammond, —Islamic Caliphate a Dream, not Reality," *Middle East Online*, December 13, 2006, http://www.middle-east-online.com/english/?id=18746 (accessed May 7, 2011).

were those associated with the league of imperialism hindered the development of China's productive forces.[145] The Taliban described corruption as those vices and entities that caused a departure from the true teachings of the Prophet Mohammed.[146] The ideology looked to —end mischief in the country and oust leaders who are devoted to self-centered positional power."[147] Like Mao, the Taliban rejected classes of society linked to exploitative Western powers. Afghan intellectuals and technocrats were rejected since the Taliban considered them products of a Western or Soviet-style education.[148] Although sharia was primarily used to run the *Khelafat*, its dual purpose was to institute a system enforcing purity and absence of corrupt practices.

Analogous Ideological Mechanisms

Both ideologies possessed analogous components. Maoism and Taliban ideology are both distinct culturally, but possessed similarities in their oppressor-oppressed dialectic, a driving vanguard body, and a way to mobilize and indoctrinate. This was a broad analysis, but was needed to realize the universality of mass mobilization and the need for levels of competent leadership in order to conduct revolutionary operations successfully.

---

[145]Mao, —Analysis of the Classes in Chinese Society," 1:13.

[146]Nojumi, *The Rise of the Taliban in Afghanistan:Mass Mobilization, Civil War, and the Future of the Region*, 154. —Anyone who refuses to obey the Ameer-ul-mumineen will be called a rebel according to sharia and requirement to execute them."

[147]Ibid.

[148]Rashid, *Taliban:Militant Islam, Oil and Fundamentalism in Central Asia*, 97.

Mao explained that the proletariat was oppressed by a bourgeoisie, the landowning class that controls a workers livelihood. The bourgeoisie were linked to imperialistic powers like the merchant or comprador class.[149] According to Mao, this bourgeoisie class exploited both China's progress and had already performed unfair actions against the peasant class. In the Taliban's dialectic, the oppressed were members of the Taliban and the all qualified Muslims willing to participate in jihad. The oppressor in the Taliban's dialectic were warlords, corrupt puppet governments, and Western countries seeking to weaken the Islamic extremist movement. In Maoism, the CCP was steered by the proletariat. As mentioned earlier, this is one characteristic that digressed from traditional Communism. The Taliban movement had a religious-based vanguard. The khalifah acted as the determinant of the revolution's direction. Ultimate decisions came from the amir, Mullah Omar.

Both movements had means to indoctrinate and recruit soldiers to support the revolution. The CCP stood up various peasant associations to mobilize the force structure required to fight against the bourgeoisie. The Taliban relied on a madrassas spread across the Afghan-Pakistan border to recruit, indoctrinate, and train young men in support the jihad movement against oppressors.

Parallel's Purpose

The correlation between various groups in both movements served to understand how Maoism can be used to gain insights on the Taliban strategy. The parallels gave credence to the suggested vulnerabilities gathered from further data collection and

---

[149]Mao, "Analysis of the Classes in Chinese Society," 1:13.

analysis. There were similarities in the timing both movements arose. These historical similarities resulted in Mao and Omar to seek a common type of endstate. Within each ideology were components that provided a generally similar function to conduct revolutionary operations. One action common to both revolutionary movements was executing mass mobilization effectively.

A Suggested Taliban Vulnerability Using Mao's Protracted War

Mao outlined in ―On Protracted War" how a weaker military power such as China could defeat the more powerful Imperial Japanese army. According to Mao, three conditions needed to be met to accomplish a successful protracted war. These conditions consisted of maintaining a united front, the gaining of international support, and the loss of the enemy's home-based support.

First, China needed to sustain a strong united front against the enemy. Mao predicted growing Chinese resentment following a decision to proceed in fighting against the invading Imperial Japanese.[150] Mao anticipated large numbers of casualties and a constant shortage of materials and weapons compared to the enemy. The Chinese needed to maintain a united front regardless of these setbacks. Mao stated that ―the united front must be persevered in; only by persevering in the united front can we persevere in

---

[150]Mao, ―On Protracted War," 2:130.

war."[151] Fortunately, there was unprecedented unity among the Chinese political groups.[152] The KMT and the CCP joined forces to form a united front.

China also required a large amount of international support for its resistance to succeed. Gaining international support isolated Imperial Japan politically, and caused neighboring countries to see the invasion as illegitimate.[153] Mao anticipated that Japan's isolation forced the country to reevaluate its actions in order to avoid further damage of its country's reputation. Fortunately, China gained international support throughout its resistance against Imperial Japan.

Third, Imperial Japan needed to experience a lack of internal support. Continued deployment of Japanese forces degraded the country's support for the Chinese invasion. Moreover, the economic strain the war compounded internal resentment against the war. Increased casualties coupled with long troop deployments from home contributed to growing Japanese opposition. Mao expected this condition to occur and played a factor in leading the Japanese to seek a compromise.

A caveat to China achieving these three conditions laid in the timing of when these conditions occurred. Mao did not know how long the protracted war against the Japanese would last. According to Mao, strategic success depended on maintaining a

---

[151]Ibid., 2:154. —To win victory, we must persevere in the War of Resistance, in the united front and in the protracted war."

[152]Snow, *Red Star Over China,* xxvi. In July 1937, an agreement was signed for joint Nationalist-Communist war of resistance against Japan. Pg 23 On Protracted War Mao stated —To win victory, and yet neglect political mobilization is like wishing to —go south by driving the chariot north" and the result would inevitably be to forfeit victory.

[153]Mao, —On Protracted War," 2:139. —Widespread guerrilla warfare and people's anti-war sentiment will wear down this big Japanese Force."

united front long enough for the other two conditions to occur.[154] In order to defeat and destroy the forces of Japan, Mao believed that the unity of China was the most important of the three conditions.[155]

Suggested Taliban Vulnerabilities in Mass Mobilization

Mass mobilization was the ―method through which a centralized political organization attempts to implement widespread changes in a society.‖[156] Socially, mass mobilization created a new structure by modifying and breaking the theoretical borders between social classes.[157] If a revolutionary movement failed to accomplish widespread mass mobilization, a movement was ineffective because there was no acting group.

Mass mobilization requires a phase of mass organization and mass participation. These phases are interchangeable.[158] Mass organization occurs when the population forms groups. Mass participation on the other hand was the point when either individuals or organizations attempt to cause changes in within their own social class.

---

[154]Ibid., 2:142. ―It should be reiterated that the change from inferiority to superiority and the completion of preparations for the counter-offensive will involve three things. Namely an increase in China's own strength, increase in Japan's difficulties, and increase in international support.‖

[155]Ibid., 2:117. ―Three conditions are required to defeat and destroy the forces of Japan: first, the establishment of an anti-Japanese Front in China; second, the formation of an international anti-Japanese united front; third, the rise of the revolutionary movement of the people in Japan and the Japanese colonies. The unity of China is the most important of the three.

[156]Nojumi, *The Rise of the Taliban in Afghanistan*: *Mass Mobilization, Civil War, and the Future of the Region*, 11. Much of the background on mass mobilization theory came from this book in Chapter Two The Theory of Mass Mobilization.

[157]Ibid., 11.

[158]Ibid., 13.

The scale of mass mobilization relied on the numbers of those involved in mass participation. In *Investigation of a Peasant Revolt in Hunan Province,* Mao emphasized the importance in using peasants to institute social reform. In relation to mass mobilization theory, it was clear that one of the main reasons he selected the peasant population carry out revolution was for its sheer numbers.[159] Mao expressed this point by saying ―This astonishing and accelerating rate of expansion explained why the local tyrants, evil gentry and corrupt officials have been isolated, why the public has been amazed at how completely the world has changed since the peasant movement.‖[160]

Yet in a segment of the report entitled ―Vanguards of the Revolution,‖ Mao separated the peasants into three distinct groups. These groups were the rich, the middle, and the poor. He considered the willingness of these groups to participate in national revolution. For instance, Mao generalized that the rich peasant would ―generally enter the name of some sixty or seventy year-old member of the family for they are in constant dread of conscription. After joining, the rich peasants are not keen on doing any work for the peasant association. They remain inactive throughout.‖[161] According to Mao it was the poor peasant that had always ―been the main force in the bitter fight and the most responsive to Communist Party leadership.‖[162] Mao revealed an important consideration

---

[159]Mao, ―Report On An Investigation of the Peasant Movement in Hunan, 1:33. ―Without the poor peasant class, it would have been impossible to bring about the present revolutionary situation in the countryside or to overthrow the local tyrants and evil gentry and complete the democratic revolution.‖

[160]Ibid., 1:35.

[161]Ibid., 1:31.

[162]Ibid., 1:32.

that impacted mass participation and in turn affected mass mobilization. This consideration was what specific group of people in the population was capable and willing to mass participate.

This same concept in mass participation could be applied to the Taliban. A majority of the Taliban's fighters were Pashtun.[163] In addition, the Pashtun made up forty-two percent of Afghanistan's population.[164] This was the largest ethnic group in Afghanistan. Having the support of the population's majority does not in itself cause social change automatically. But through application of Mao's logic, the number of Taliban fighters needed to be large enough to overwhelm any opposition. Thus, to implement national revolution, it would be logical to mobilize as much of the Pashtun population as possible.

The Taliban's fighting force was not made up of hardcore Islamic extremists. The Taliban were a conglomeration of five distinct groups. These groups consisted of the purely ideologically driven madrassa students, genuine jihadist recruits provided by local village mullahs, various local allies and opportunists, and mercenaries.[165] The first two groups were considered hardcore followers of Taliban ideology. Of these groups, those fighting fell between twenty to twenty-five years of age with Taliban commanders in

---

[163]Rashid, *Taliban: Militant Islam, Oil and Fundamentalism in Central Asia*, 90. Rashid mentions that JUI formed inside the Pashtun belt in the Northwest Frontier Province (NWFP). It also gained influence over these southern Pashtuns. JUI formed the original Taliban organization.

[164]CIA World Factbook, ―Afghanistan,‖ https://www.cia.gov/library/publications/ the-world-factbook/geos/af.html (accessed May 7, 2011).

[165]Giustozzi, *Koran, Kalashnikov and Laptop*, 42.

their thirties and forties.[166] Therefore, Mao revealed a possible vulnerability in the area of mass participation. The Taliban required specific types of committed fighters numerous enough to participate actively in revolutionary actions.

Mass organization involved bringing participants together into groups. The mass organization phase was also critical in achieving successful mass mobilization. However, mass organization was not limited to only the Pashtun population. There were several groups in Afghanistan that achieved mass organization. These groups included the Taliban's allies to such as Hizb-i-Islami, the Haqqani Network, and a small core of foreign Al-Qaeda militants operating in Afghanistan.[167] Rival political groups included the Northern Alliance.

Thus, several political groups formed in Afghanistan since the Soviet invasion. The very existence of various political groups suggested a second vulnerability to the Taliban strategy. If the Taliban looked to establish a united IEA in Afghanistan, then it would require unification of these political groups, according to its ideology. By unifying groups, both allies and rivals would need submit to the Taliban's sharia law and its *Khelafat*. In addition, the Taliban would need to find a way to bridge differences among non-Pashtun groups and find common issues capable of bringing them together. Yet since 1994, many non-Pashtun groups like those in the Northern alliance have been opposed to

---

[166]Ibid., 38.

[167]Jane's: Defence and Security Intelligence and Insurgency Center, Taliban, Alliances and Rivalries, http://jtic.janes.com.ezproxy6.ndu.edu/JDIC/JTIC/document View.do?docId=/content1/janesdata/binder/jwit/jwit0270.htm@current&pageSelected=al lJanes&keyword=Taliban&backPath=http://jtic.janes.com.ezproxy6.ndu.edu/JDIC/JTIC/ search&Prod_Name=&activeNav=/JDIC/JTIC#toclink-j351196161274956774714 (accessed May 7, 2011).

the Pashtun-heavy Taliban not only for political reasons, but for ethnic reasons as well. Therefore, this circumstance indicated that any meaningful unification in the short term seemed unlikely.[168] If the Taliban were unable to achieve unity, then it placed the strategic goal of establishing the IEA in jeopardy.

Vulnerability For Taliban Maintaining Its Own United Internal Front

Mao's writings "On Protracted War" suggested an additional vulnerability of maintaining cohesion internal to the organization. The Taliban's organization was a network of franchises.[169] This network had both ideologically motivated cadres, and smaller militant cells "that are sometimes in harmony with the Taliban's objectives."[170] These militant cells used the Taliban label for their local aims in return for support and cooperation.[171] The cell was then expected to follow the strategic directives of the Taliban leadership. This decentralized operation suggested a possible vulnerability.

Defections from the Taliban were not prevalent, but did occur. They indicated instability inside the Taliban's organizational structure. *Newsweek* reported that more than a thousand fighters had walked away recently from the Taliban insurgency over the past several months. The one thousand defectors did so as a result of seeing heavy losses

---

[168] Ali A. Jalali, "Wither the Taliban?," Foreign Military Office, 6 March 1999, http://fmso.leavenworth.army.mil/documents/taliban.htm (accessed May 8, 2011).

[169] Afsar, "The Evolution of the Taliban," 50.

[170] Ibid.

[171] Ibid.

from intense fighting.[172] In 2010, a total of sixty-four of the Taliban's members had defected to the local government.[173]

The Taliban's leadership is divided into three groups. These groups are the conservatives, the moderates, and the religious police.[174] The conservative group is composed of those loyal to Mullah Omar and come from traditionalists. The moderate group had a more pragmatic approach to developing and running the IEA. The moderates were more flexible when it came to issues concerning women, and believed there needed to be a parliamentary apparatus to incorporate the concerns of various political and ethnic groups when developing edicts directing proper Islamic living.[175] The third group is the religious police under the organization of Promotion of Virtue and Prevention of Vice. This was an independent organization that implemented sharia law according its own interpretations of Islamic law. The religious police are closer to the conservatives in their beliefs.

---

[172]Sami Yousafzai, ―How the Taliban Lost Its Swagger; Disgusted by the insurgency's relentless brutality, more than 1000 fighters have walked away in recent month," *Newsweek*, March 7, 2011, http://proquest.umi.com.lumen.cgsccarl.com pqdweb?index=0&did=2281572621&SrchMode=1&sid=1&Fmt=3&VInst=PROD&VTy pe=PQD&RQT=309&VName=PQD&TS=1306012219&clientId=5094 (accessed May 7, 2011).

[173]Jane's: Defence and Security Intelligence and Analysis, Event Database, http://jtic.janes.com.ezproxy6.ndu.edu/JDIC/JTIC/search/advSearchResults.do?searchTer m=Taliban+AND+defect&searchTermOption=Full+Text&startPostDate=&endPostDate =&regionCountry=All+Regions+%26+Countries&dataSetSub=All+Groups&resultsToDi splay=20&sort=Score-false&pageSelected=janesReference&type=advSearchResults (accessed April 15, 2011).

[174]Nojumi, *The Rise of the Taliban in Afghanistan:Mass Mobilization, Civil War, and the Future of the Region*, 179.

[175]Ibid.

Internal disputes between the Taliban's conservative and moderate members occurred on issues such as dealing with women's roles, methods to preserve popular support, and the power arrangements of the IEA. For example, the conservatives and moderates debated on whether the IEA should allow women doctors and nurses to work in hospitals. Another instance illustrates a split in the Taliban leadership over ways to build a more positive image. The Taliban were split in regards to the use of suicide bombings due to the effect it had on civilian casualties and the organization's popular support.[176] Conflicts over the power-sharing arrangements with those Afghan political groups that could not be defeated militarily have also occurred. In order to solve this, moderates believed that the Taliban needed to explore ways to establish a viable administration that would serve the interests of all groups in Afghanistan.[177]

There are two instances where groups broke off of the main Taliban movement. In 2002, Jamiat-i-Khundam-ul Koran split from the Taliban in efforts to form a party of moderates, but was unable to rally enough support during parliamentary elections.[178] In 2003, a controversy existed in the Taliban on whether an intensification of the insurgency was required. As a result a faction named Jaish-ul Muslimeen quit the Taliban in

---

[176]Guistozzi, *Koran, Kalashnikov and Laptop: The Neo-Taliban Insurgency in Afghanistan*, 117.

[177]Nojumi, *The Rise of the Taliban in Afghanistan:Mass Mobilization, Civil War, and the Future of the Region*, 180.

[178]Guistozzi, *Koran, Kalashnikov and Laptop: The Neo-Taliban Insurgency in Afghanistan*, 82.

September 2003.[179] One year later, the Jaish organization returned back to the Taliban.[180] These instances indicate fissures in the organization.

Vulnerability For Taliban Gaining Positive International Support

According to Mao, winning protracted war relied primarily on maintaining a solid united front against the enemy. In addition, China required a level of international support. International support provided China additional political strength when they fought the Japanese. This was the second pillar necessary to achieve strategic victory. This same concept is relevant to the Taliban's strategy.

The rigid viewpoints of the senior Taliban's leadership and their unwillingness to compromise on human rights issues have marred the movement's chances to gain the kind of international support Mao prescribed. In 1996 the United Nations' Children Fund suspended education programs in Herat because girls were excluded. This suspension did not deter the Taliban.[181] Again in 1996, United Nations Secretary submitted protest statements after massive media coverage of the Taliban's hanging of former President Najibullah and the treatment of Kabul's women.[182] These protests also met with no Taliban response.[183] These instances were examples of how the Taliban's lack of compromise led to negative perceptions by the international community.

---

[179]Ibid., 81.

[180]Ibid.

[181]Rashid, *Taliban: Militant Islam, Oil and Fundamentalism in Central Asia*, 113.

[182]Ibid.

[183]Ibid.

Another issue that dampens the Taliban's chances to gain international support is its reliance on opium. Farming of opium to earn revenue for the Taliban movement has also been looked down upon by the international community. Opium production constituted thirty percent of Afghanistan's gross domestic product.[184] Before 2001, organizations like the United Nations' Office on Drugs and Crime worked with the Taliban to find alternate viable crop substitutes. Yet based on the country's dependence on opium to build revenue, progress has been slow. Opium production hinders the Taliban from gaining much needed international support in order to win protracted war.

Furthermore, the Taliban's intolerance in abiding to mainstream Islamic norms and the Shia population, isolated the Taliban from countries like Iran and Saudi Arabia. In 1997, during the invasion of Mazar the Taliban decided to ―cleanse the north of Shia."[185] As a result, United Nations estimate that between 6,000 to 8,000 Shia were killed.[186] The Taliban also detained and executed Iranian diplomats during its Taliban attack. This action infuriated Tehran, and worsened an already tense relationship between Iran and the Taliban. Saudi Arabia and the Taliban became tense in regards to the release of Osama bin Laden in 2001. In the Saudi perspective, the refusal by Mullah Omar to hand over Osama bin Laden undermined the authority of its Royal Family.[187] As a result,

---

[184]Farhana Schmidt,―FromIslamic Warriors to Drug Lords: The Evolution of the Taliban Insurgency," *Mediterranean Quarterly* (Spring 2010), http://web.ebscohost.com. lumen.cgsccarl.com/ehost/pdfviewer/pdfviewer?sid=647c5a1f-02de-42c3-9556-51c514d338c6%40sessionmgr12&vid=30&hid=24 (accessed May 2, 2011).

[185]Rashid, *Taliban: Militant Islam, Oil and Fundamentalism in Central Asia*, 74.

[186]Ibid.

[187]Ibid., 211.

this perceived insult caused Saudi leaders to eventually stop any support, and further isolate the Taliban from the world community.[188]

Therefore, the Taliban's absence of strong international support presented a possible vulnerability. Without international support, the means to win protracted war may disappear. The Taliban have attempted to justify its intolerance by its interpretations of sharia. These interpretations were not palatable with the international community to include neighboring Islamic states like Iran and Saudi Arabia. If the Taliban looked to win its revolutionary war politically, then the organization had to find ways to bolster outside support.

Analysis of Taliban Strategy Using Maoist Contradiction

Based on its strategy, the Taliban desired to ―end mischief in the country, establish peace, and security, to protect life, wealth and honor and enforce the sharia, do jihad against leaders who are devoted for power and endeavor to make the land of Afghanistan an exemplary state."[189] After the Taliban took control of most of Afghanistan, they implemented their own version of sharia law in order to run the country. The body that enforced Mullah Omar edicts was the Department of the Promotion of Virtue and Prevention of Vice. The organization had thousands of young men recruited with minimum madrassa education, and derived numerous edicts from their interpretation of sharia.[190] These edicts covered every aspect of social behavior for

---

[188]Nojumi, *The Rise of the Taliban in Afghanistan:Mass Mobilization, Civil War, and the Future of the Region*, 189.

[189]Ibid., 154.

[190]Rashid, *Taliban: Militant Islam, Oil and Fundamentalism in Central Asia*, 106.

the population.[191] The contradictions of disobedience to obedience were achieved by the use of religious police. Yet there were instances where enforcing the edicts took the highest priority.

There were several accounts where the Taliban used sharia law to resolve a single contradiction while disregarding others. For example, there was one instance where a widow was unable to earn money because women were not allowed to work. The religious police did not consider handling other types of contradictions such as suffering and non-suffering. Hence this particular lady became a beggar instead of working in the bakery where she was previously employed.[192] Obedience to the published rules superseded other unconsidered contradictions.

Another example dealt with economics where the Taliban forbade the taking of interests on loans. Regardless of interest being the bedrock of the modern banking system, the Taliban rejected it.[193] In this case rather than consider the contradiction that interest solves, the Taliban reverted to a literal interpretation to achieve blind obedience to Islamic law.

The use of Mao's concept of contradiction suggested a vulnerability in the way the Taliban designed their overall strategy. These preceding vignettes illustrated the Taliban's focus on resolving only one particular contradiction. Mao's strategy sought to resolve the contradiction between the oppressed and the oppressor through national

---

[191]Ibid., 107.

[192]Ibid., 108.

[193]Juan R. I. Cole, ―The Taliban Women, and the Hegelian Private Sphere,‖ in *The Taliban and the Crisis in Afghanistan*, ed. Robert D. Crews and Amin Tarzi (Cambridge: Harvard University Press, 2008), 133.

revolution. The Taliban seeks to work out the contradiction between disobedience and obedience through sharia law.

The use of Mao's contradiction concepts connoted that this same thought process was being applied by the Taliban in its revolutionary military actions. The Taliban's strategy could be looked at as too military focused based on the organization's interpretations to carry out jihad. This focus on following sharia strictly for the sake of resolving a particular contradiction may have caused the Taliban to ignore reestablishing governmental institutions, and the true needs of the population. This tendency to disregard other important contradictions deliberately and oversimplify social problems poses a possible vulnerability in the Taliban's strategy.

<u>Analysis of Taliban Strategy Using Maoist Dialectical Materialism</u>

Mao's "On Dialectical Materialism" provided insights to the idealistic nature of the Taliban's strategy. The Taliban's ideology is dedicated to the implementation and enforcement of its strict Deobandi form of sharia.[194] Mao stated that "philosophical idealism and religious theology derives from their denial of the unity and material nature of the world, and is a result of the action of spirit."[195] The idealist philosopher George Fredrich Hegel held that the present world resulted from the development of the so-called

---

[194]Jane's Defence and Security Site, Taliban, Key Facts, http://jtic.janes.com.ez proxy6.ndu.edu/JDIC/JTIC/documentView.do?docId=/content1/janesdata/binder/jwit/jwi t0270.htm@current&pageSelected=allJanes&keyword=Taliban&backPath=http://jtic.jan es.com.ezproxy6.ndu.edu/JDIC/JTIC/search&Prod_Name=&activeNav=/JDIC/JTIC (accessed December 15, 2011).

[195]Mao, "Dialectical Materialism," 188.

―world idea."[196] Based on Mao's definition, sharia fell under the category of idealism, because it was derived from an institution that separated movement from matter.

Taliban ideology placed ―consciousness, spirit, or concepts in place of objective reality."[197] The Taliban leadership demonstrated idealism through its correspondence as well as its approach in establishing federal institutions. For example, the head of the Department of Religious Observances, Maulvi Qalamuddin stated ―We fought for sharia and now this is the organization that will implement it. I will implement it come what may."[198] He implies that sharia was the first priority regardless of the physical economic and social ramifications. Another example demonstrated how idealism affected the building of federal institutions. After the capture of Kabul, the Taliban shut down sixty-three schools affecting 103,000 girls since it was against the principles of perfect Islam.[199]

The Taliban's abilities to make decisions and plan off an idealistic strategy hinted at a potential vulnerability, because the Taliban's strategy placed higher priority on something intangible. Therefore, the ideology was more prone to disregard the material condition of the country. Mao's dialectical materialism essay suggested the Taliban

---

[196]Ibid.

[197]Ibid., 183.

[198]Rashid, *Taliban: Militant Islam, Oil and Fundamentalism in Central Asia*, 106.

[199]Ibid., 108.

strategy was prone to remain static and less conducive to change since the idealistic

principles it used to guide its strategy were rigid and immobile.[200]

---

[200]Mao, "Dialectical Materialism," 189. Mao states that the idealist view the basic nature of the universe and society was eternally unchanging.

CHAPTER 5

CONCLUSIONS

To understand Mao's approach, it was important to comprehend the original intent behind the ideology's formation. After years of exploitation and unfair economic practices by the Western regimes, and a series of internal battles, the Chinese people were frustrated. The Qing Dynasty had collapsed, and the country fell into a political vacuum. Mao believed a fundamental change was required in the country. He believed the change required a total revision of the social structure of China. In his opinion it was this structure of social classes that caused China to fall into ruin.[201] Mao adopted Leninism, because it was an available plan that provided a means to implement social change.[202] Yet Mao could not merely reapply Lenin's specific principles to China, he needed to modify them in order to fit China's circumstances. Thus, he adopted Leninism for its essence and its basic dialectic.[203]

Lenin's dialectic was between the proletariat and bourgeoisie. These were two economic groups that Lenin believed were contradictions to one another. Lenin's goals were to merge these classes through armed revolution in preparation for entering a stage of socialism followed by a utopian communist stage. When Mao adopted the dialectic, he

---

[201]Mao, ―Analysis of the Classes in Chinese Society,‖ 1:13. ―Landlord and comprador class existence is utterly incompatible with the aims of the Chinese Revolution.‖

[202]Greiss, *The Arab Israeli War, The Chinese Civil War, and the Korean War*, 37.

[203]Schram, *Political Thought of Mao Tse Tung*, 55.

71

modified it to landlord and peasant.[204] Altering the ideology in this fashion was a wise

decision in forming the CCP.

By changing the core dialectic, he was capable of tapping into the largest segment

of China's population at the time. In ―Dialectical Materialism,‖ Mao dubbed the peasants

as the true materialists and therefore the only group that could alter the course of China's

history. In ―On Contradiction,‖ Mao again reinforced the point that it was the peasant

who was the polar opposite of the landowning class.[205] ―Report on An Investigation of

the Peasant Movement in Hunan Province,‖ convinced him that his idea's of peasant led

revolution were possible as well as potentially powerful to leverage other classes because

of sheer numbers and the peasants' ability to organize themselves.[206]

Mao centered his ideology around the peasant population. Incorporating peasants

caused his strategic goals to divert away from Lenin's, and transform into nationalistic

ones. Mao sought a regaining of China's stature. The Communist's approach to

revolution was an aggressive enough means to accomplish this. Mass mobilization

became the key concept for Mao to conduct a successful revolution. Yet mass

mobilization was not simply the gathering of peasants. It was determined through the

research that mass mobilization was multi-facted and that the decision to conduct mass

organization and participation came with some considerations. Some of these

considerations dealt with mobilizing the right people willing to fulfill the ideologies

---

[204]Mao, ―Analysis of the Classes in Chinese Society,‖ 1:13. ―Landlord and comprador class existence is utterly incompatible with the aims of the Chinese Revolution.‖

[205]Mao, ―On Contradiction,‖ 1:323.

[206]Mao, ―Report on an Investigation of the Peasant Movement in Hunan,‖ 1:24.

vision. Another consideration from "Vanguards of the Revolution," was knowing that with mass mobilization came followers with varied levels of commitment. All mass participants were not necessarily willing to participate in armed revolution.[207]

Rather than mobilize a smaller portion that could fight, Mao placed more focus on the peasant population as whole. This was because the true purpose of conducting mass mobilization was for its political effects. Organizing the peasant population was a political statement that supported the core of his ideology. By successfully mobilizing them, he validated the first steps towards his vision to rival factions especially the KMT. This validation threatened the survival of the KMT, because Mao's movement gave peasants the perception that the KMT represented everything that caused China's past failures. The KMT were corrupt and a proxy for the Western powers that oppressed the country.

The Imperial Japanese invasion in 1937 was in many cases fortunate for Mao's cause, because it was the one event that could mass mobilize and unite all the groups in China.[208] The invasion forced rivals to come together into a _united front' in order to withstand the forces of Japanese imperialism. The invasion caused unprecedented unity among the two warring factions. This was where the research found the most significant findings.

The actualization of the "united front" held the key in winning the war against the Japanese. Mao knew that the China was inferior to the Japanese in all aspects except for

---

[207]Ibid., 1:31.

[208]Greiss, *The Arab Israeli Wars, The Chinese Civil War, and the Korean War,* 49.

population. This was why the united front was so important. It was one of the only advantages the Chinese had, but in order to use it properly, Mao stated in *On Protracted War*, that the united front was a political maneuver analogous to the rallying of the peasants earlier in the Chinese Civil War.[209]

The united front and mass mobilization go hand in hand. Thus protracted war and mass mobilization are inextricable from one another. They are inextricable because the united front made the three phases of revolutionary action work. To Mao mass mobilization gave him the three things he needed to win protracted war. These things were domestic popular support, a tool to campaign his cause to the international community, and a means to physically exhaust the enemy. These three elements incorporated the concept of mass mobilization and, revealed it as the fundamental requirement to winning protracted war and revolution.

Mass mobilization had a political message that accompanied it. In relation to protracted war, mobilization symbolized a population that was in full accord, and willing to defend itself. Such a message not only fulfilled the requirement for domestic support, but it also politicized the movement to the international community. Gaining international support was necessary, since it contributed to the political isolation of the enemy.

Mass mobilization also played a crucial role in physically exhausting the enemy. This particular function of mass mobilization required the most attention because it required a delicate balance between physically exhausting the enemy by military means while still preserving the force to sustain the domestic and international support. Ironically, using mass mobilization to physically exhaust the enemy was not the sole

---

[209]Mao, ─On Protracted War," 2:123.

means to victory. It was the political purpose behind it. To Mao, attriting Imperial Japanese soldiers itself did not bring about a strategic Chinese victory. The Japanese government and its indigenous population needed to feel the effects the Imperial Japanese army endured. Whether these effects were economical, military, or political did not matter. What mattered was the Japanese decision to withdraw and shape the nation's psyche into thinking that its military actions were no longer worth the sacrifice.

Mao did not know when that point would be. All the CCP could do was keep the organization alive, and garner the support that came with staying alive. The mission was to maintain cohesion long enough using mass mobilization as the political tool until the Imperial Japanese capitulated politically from its inability to fully legitimize its efforts because of resulting isolation and lack of Japanese popular support. As a result, the importance of Chinese mass mobilization to attain victory was validated.

So after realizing the importance of mass mobilization in China's Civil War and its engagement against the Japanese, its vulnerabilities were applied to the Taliban's strategy both before and after they lost power of Afghanistan in 2001. Mass mobilization was applicable in both cases. As a result, insights were gained on possible vulnerabilities within the Taliban's organization.

The research first looked into the effects the Taliban ideology had on mass mobilization. Unlike Mao, the core contradiction within its ideology was not focused on the physical concerns of the population as a whole. The contradiction was not centered around a designated economic social class, it was a religious contradiction in the realm of disobedience to obedience, to god in turn the IEA. The ideology's targeted audience looked to assemble those that could help renew the glory of the Islamic state. The Taliban looking to be the executor of gathering support for the movement struggled with ethnic and political limitations. Fortunately for the Taliban, most of them were familiar with Pashtunwali politics and could maneuver themselves brokering deals to achieve mass mobilization with other means if required.[210] Other irreconcilable non-Pashtun groups were forced to abide to Taliban ideology through the religious police. These actions indicated that mass participation and organization to support the Taliban ideology was forced upon them and did not receive the committed response Mao's ideology managed to achieve. This suggested a possible vulnerability in the Taliban to mass mobilize enough people to form a large enough force to implement its own version of protracted war.

The study also revealed the already existing mobilization within the Taliban organization has the potential to falter. Even prior to its loss of power, hardline, and moderate Taliban leadership were conflicted on the course of actions necessary to rebuild the country under the *Khelafat*.[211] These differences led to groups splitting away from the mainline Taliban hoping to implement their own changes. Yet these groups like Jamiat-i-Khundam-ul Koran and Jaish-ul-Muslimeen also suffered problems maintaining a strong hold of supporters and a unified effort. The formation of such groups demonstrated that the united front of the Taliban is liable to breaking apart occasionally.

---

[210]Abdulkader Sinno, ―Explaining the Taliban's Ability to Mobilize the Pashtuns," in *The Taliban and the Crisis of Afghanistan*, ed. Robert D. Crews and Amin Tarzi (Cambridge: Harvard University Press, 2008), 78.

[211]Nojumi, *The Rise of the Taliban in Afghanistan:Mass Mobilization, Civil War, and the Future of the Region*, 82.

In the realm of protracted war is where other vulnerabilities lie. The Taliban have attempted to conduct protracted war with its fragile alliance. The Maoist revolutionary approach suggests that the Taliban may be far from achieving strategic victory because of its inability to gain the international support for its cause. Prior to losing power in Afghanistan, the Taliban had already had marginal worldwide support for its perceived abuses of sharia. In 2001, only Pakistan, Saudi Arabia, and the United Arab Emirates recognized them as an official state.[212] Nongovernmental organizations and the United Nations had documented a less than favorable relationship with the Taliban regime. The Taliban's struggle to gain the overwhelming support Mao prescribes as fundamental in winning protracted war.

Thus, the research provides two major insights on Taliban vulnerabilities. The findings suggest that the Taliban need to find a way to modify its rigid ideology in order to build stronger cohesion if it desires to achieve the levels of mass mobilization necessary to achieve victory. In addition, the research finds that if the Taliban desires to isolate the United States and its allies internationally, one of the first steps requires a significant change in the movement's attitude toward human rights. Improving the movement's international image would also include an attempt to normalize its relationship with other countries such as Iran and Saudi Arabia. Yet after having looked at the trends, building such relationship and isolating the United States and its allies is unlikely.

---

[212]Country Watch Afghanistan, ‒Foreign Relations," http://www.countrywatch.com.lumen.cgsccarl.com/cw_topic.aspx?type=text&vcountry=1&topic=POFOR (accessed May 2, 2011).

BIBLIOGRAPHY

Books

Cahn, Steven M. *Classics of Political and Moral Philosophy*. 4th ed. New York: Oxford University Press, 2002.

Cole, Juan R. I. "The Taliban Women, and the Hegelian Private Sphere." In *The Taliban and the Crisis of Afghanistan*, edited by Robert D. Crews and Amin Tarzi, 118-154. Cambridge: Harvard University Press, 2008.

Crews, Robert D., and Amin Tarzi, eds. *The Taliban and the Crisis of Afghanistan*. Cambridge: Harvard University Press, 2008.

Dreyer, Edward L. "Continuity and Change." In *A Military History of China*, edited by David A. Graff and Robin Higham, 19-38. Cambridge: Westview Press, 2002.

Ewans, Martin. *Afghanistan: A Short History of Its People and Politics.* New York: HarperCollins, 2002.

Giustozzi, Antonio. *Koran, Kalashnikov and Laptop: The Neo-Taliban Insurgency in Afghanistan.* New York: Columbia University Press, 2008.

Graff, David A., and Robin Higham, eds. *A Military History of China.* Cambridge: Westview Press, 2002.

Greiss, Thomas. *The Arab Israeli Wars, The Chinese Civil War, and the Korean War.* Wayne: Avery Publishing Group, 1987.

Macridis, Roy C. *Contemporary Political Ideologies: Movements and Regimes.* Cambridge: Winthrop Publishers, 1980.

MacKinnon, Stephen R. "The Sino-Japanese Conflict." In *A Military History of China*, edited by David A. Graff and Robin Higham, 211-228. Cambridge: Westview Press, 2002.

Mao Tse Tung. *Selected Works of Mao Tse Tung.* 2 Vol. Peking: Foreign Languages Press, 1967.

———. "Analysis of the Classes in Chinese Society." In *Selected Works of Mao Tse Tung.* 1:13-22. Peking: Foreign Languages Press, 1967.

———. "Dialectical Materialism." In *The Political Thought of Mao Tse Tung*, 185-194. New York: Praeger, 1970.

———. ―On Contradiction." In *Selected Works of Mao Tse Tung*, 1:311-345. Peking: Foreign Languages Press, 1967.

———. ―On Practice." In *Selected Works of Mao Tse Tung*, 1:295-310. Peking: Foreign Languages Press, 1967.

———. ―On Protracted War." In *Selected Works of Mao Tse Tung*, 2:113-188. Peking Foreign Languages Press, 1967.

———. ―Problems of Strategy in Guerrilla War Against Japan." In *Selected Works of Mao Tse Tung*, 2:79-109. Peking: Foreign Languages Press, 1967.

———. ―Report on an Investigation of the Peasant Movement in Hunan." In *Selected Works of Mao Tse Tung*, 1:23-55. Peking: Foreign Languages Press, 1967.

———. ―To the Glory of the Hans." In *The Political Thought of Mao Tse Tung*, 161-168. New York: Praeger, 1970.

Meisner, Maurice. *Mao's China*. London: Collier, Macmillan Publishers, 1977.

Nojumi, Neamatollah. *The Rise of the Taliban in Afghanistan:Mass Mobilization, Civil War, and the Future of the Region*. New York: Palgrave, 2002.

———. ―The Rise and Fall of the Taliban," In *The Taliban and the Crisis of Afghanistan*, edited by Robert D. Crews and Amin Tarzi, 90-117. Cambridge: Westview Press, 2008.

Rashid, Ahmed. *Taliban: Militant Islam, Oil and Fundamentalism in Central Asia*. New Haven: Yale University Press, 2010.

Rejai, Mostafa. *Political Ideologies: A Comparative Approach*. Armonk: M.E. Sharpe, 1995.

Schram, Stuart R. *Mao Tse Tung*. Baltimore: Penguin Books, 1974.

———. *The Political Thought of Mao Tse-tung*. New York: Praeger, 1970.

Schurman, Franz, and Orville Schell, eds. *The China Reader: Communist China*. New York: Vintage Books, 1967.

Sinno, Abdulkader. ―Explaining the Taliban's Ability to Mobilize the Pashtuns." In *The Taliban and the Crisis of Afghanistan*, edited by Robert D. Crews and Amin Tarzi, 59-89. Cambridge: Harvard University Press, 2008.

Snow, Edgar. *Red Star Over China*. New York: Grove Press, 1968.

Zaeef, Abdul Salam. *My Life with the Taliban*. New York: Columbia University Press, 2010.

Journal Articles

Dorronsoro, Gilles. ―The Taliban‗s Winning Strategy in Afghanistan.‖ *Carnegie Endowment for International Peace* (2009). http://carnegieendowment.org/ files/taliban_winning_strategy.pdf (accessed September 2, 2010).

Frakt, Phyllis M. ―Mao‗s Concept of Representation.‖ *American Journal of Political Science* 23, no. 4 (November 1979):684-704. http://www.jstor.org.lumen. cgsccarl.com/stable/info/2110802?&Search=yes&searchText=Concept&searchTe xt=Mao%27s&searchText=Representation&list=hide&searchUri=%2Faction%2F doBasicSearch%3FQuery%3DMao%25E2%2580%2599s%2BConcept%2Bof%2 BRepresentation%26gw%3Djtx%26acc%3Don%26prq%3Dti%253A%2528Leni nism%2BAND%2BMarxism%2B%2BSome%2BPopulist%2BPerspectives%252 9%26Search%3DSearch%26hp%3D25%26wc%3Don&prevSearch=&item=1&ttl =562&returnArticleService=showArticleInfo (accessed April 5, 2011).

Johnson, Thomas H., and M. Chris Mason. ―Understanding the Taliban and Insurgency in Afghanistan.‖ *Orbis: A Journal of World Affairs* 51, no. 1 (Winter 2007). http://www.nps.edu/programs/ccs/docs/pubs/understanding%20the%20taliban%2 0and%20insurgency%20in%20afghanistan.pdf (accessed November 11, 2010).

Kagan, Fredrick W. ―The New Bolsheviks:Understanding Al Qaeda.‖ *American Enterprise Institute for Public Policy Research* (November 2005). http://www.ciaonet.org.lumen.cgsccarl.com/pbei/aei/nso/nso020/nso020.pdf (accessed September 20, 2010).

Katzenbach, Edward L. ―The Revolutionary Strategy of Mao Tse-Tung.‖ *Political Science Quarterly* 70, no. 3 (September 1955): 321-340. http://www.jstor.org/ stable/2145469 (accessed September 2, 2010).

Meisner, Maurice. ―Leninism and Maoism: Some Populist Perspectives on Marxism-Leninism in China.‖ *The China Quarterly*, 45 (January-March 1970): 2-36. http://www.jstore.org/stable/651881 (accessed September 22, 2010).

―――. ―The Maoist Legacy and Chinese Socialism.‖ *Asian Survey* 17, no. 11 (November 1977): 1016-1027. http://www.jstor.org/stable/2643350 (accessed April 5, 2011).

Sabet, Amr. ―Review:Untitled.‖ *British Journal of Middle Eastern Studies* 30, no. 1. http://www.jstor.org.lumen.cgsccarl.com/stable/pdfplus/3593252.pdf?accept TC=true (accessed April 5, 2011).

Schmidt, Farhana. ―From Islamic Warriors to Drug Lords: The Evolution of the Taliban Insurgency.‖ *Mediterranean Quarterly* (Spring 2010). http://web.ebscohost.com. lumen.cgsccarl.com/ehost/results?sid=927e06c9-74ac-4c2b-b4d7-f9db8f8193 ec%40sessionmgr10&vid=3&hid=19&bquery=(From+Islamic+Warriors+to+Dru g+Lords%3a+The+Evolution+of+the+Taliban+Insurgency)&bdata=JmRiPWE5a

CZkYj1idGgmZGI9bXRoJnR5cGU9MCZzaXRlPWVob3N0LWxpdmU%3d
(accessed May 2, 2011).

Wittfogel, Karl A. ―The Marxist View of China (Part 1).‖ *The China Quarterly* 11
    (1962): 1-20. http://www.jstor.org.lumen.cgsccarl.com/stable/651446?&Search=
    yes&searchText=View&searchText=1&searchText=Marxist&searchText=Part&s
    earchText=China&list=hide&searchUri=%2Faction%2FdoBasicSearch%3FQuer
    y%3DThe%2BMarxist%2BView%2Bof%2BChina%2BPart%2B1%26acc%3Don
    %26wc%3D&prevSearch=&item=1&ttl=8792&returnArticleService=show
    FullText (accessed May 4, 2011).

―――. ―The Marxist View of China (Part 2).‖ *The China Quarterly* 12 (1962): 154-169.
    http://www.jstor.org.lumen.cgsccarl.com/stable/651821?&Search=yes&searchTe
    xt=2&searchText=View&searchText=Marxist&searchText=Part&searchText=Ch
    ina&list=hide&searchUri=%2Faction%2FdoBasicSearch%3FQuery%3DThe%2B
    Marxist%2BView%2Bof%2BChina%2BPart%2B2%26acc%3Don%26wc%3Don
    &prevSearch=&item=1&ttl=8894&returnArticleService=showFullText (accessed
    May 4, 2011).

Online Mao Selected Works

Lenin, Vladimir I. ―Backward Europe and Advanced Asia.‖ *Lenin Collected Works.*
    http://www.marxist.org/archive/lenin/works/1913/may/18.htm (accessed
    September 2, 2010).

Mao, Tse Tung. ―Analysis of the Classes in Chinese Society.‖ *Selected Works of Mao Tse
    Tung.* http://www.marxists.org/reference/archive/mao/selected-works/volume-
    1/mswv1_1.htm (accessed October 14, 2010).

―――. ―Dialectical Materialism.‖ *Selected Works of Mao Tse Tung.*
    http://www.marxists.org/reference/archive/mao/selected-works/volume-
    6/mswv6_30.htm (accessed September 22, 2010).

―――. ―On Contradiction.‖ *Selected Works of Mao Tse Tung* http://www.marxists.org/
    reference/archive/mao/selected-works/volume-1/mswv1_17.htm (accessed
    October 14, 2010).

―――. ―On Practice.‖ *Selected Works of Mao Tse Tung* http://www.marxists.org/
    reference/archive/mao/selected-works/volume-1/mswv1_16.htm (accessed
    September 22, 2010).

―――. ―On Protracted War.‖ *Selected Works of Mao Tse-Tung* Vol.2
    http://www.marxists.org/reference/archive/mao/selected-works/volume-
    2/mswv2_09.htm (accessed September 22, 2010).

———. "Problems of Strategy in Guerrilla War Against Japan." *Selected Works of Mao Tse Tung* Vol. 2. http://www.marxists.org/reference/archive/mao/selected-works/volume-2/mswv2_09.htm (accessed September 22, 2010).

———. "Problems of Strategy in Guerrilla War Against Japan." *Selected Works of Mao Tse Tung* Vol. 2. http://www.marxists.org/reference/archive/mao/selected-works/volume-2/mswv2_09.htm (accessed September 22, 2010).

———. "Report on an Investigation of the Peasant Movement in Hunan." *Selected Works of Mao Tse Tung.* http://www.marxists.org/reference/archive/mao/selected-works/volume-1/mswv1_2.htm (accessed September 22, 2010).

Thesis

Asfar, Shahid, and Christopher A. Samples. "The Evolution of the Taliban." Master's Thesis, Naval Postgraduate School, 2008. http://www.dtic.mil/srch/search?searchview=d4&c=t3&changequery=1&template=%2Fdtic%2Fsearch%2Ftr%2Fresults-templatetr.html&s=1&fql=y&exact=n&xml=1&must1=and&pdfitems=&enableLemmatization=YES&q=&field1=TI&word1=The+Evolution+of+the+Taliban&must2=AND&field2=AU&word2=&must3=AND&field3=KEY&word3=&must4=AND&field4=NU&word4=&must5=AND&field5=AB&word5=&must6=AND&field6=AB&word6=&must7=AND&field7=DE&word7=&must8=AND&field8=SC&word8=&Submit=Submit+Query&newold=date&age=any&sort=-RD&n=30 (accessed May 2, 2011).

Cathell, John H. "Human Geography in the Afghanistan-Pakistan Region: Undermining the Taliban Using Traditional Pashtun Social Structures." Naval Postgraduate School, 2009. http://www.dtic.mil/cgi-bin/GetTRDoc?AD=ADA502894&Location=U2&doc=GetTRDoc.pdf (accessed May 2, 2011).

Magazine and Newspaper Articles

BBC News. "Interview with Mullah Omar-transcript." 15 November 2001. http://news.bbc.co.uk/2/hi/south_asia/1657368.stm (accessed August 30, 2010).

Bergen, Peter. "Two Arguments for What to do in Afghanistan." *Time*, October 1, 2009. http://www.peterbergen.com/services/print.aspx?id=403 (accessed March 21, 2011).

The Guardian. "Mullah Omar-in his own words." 26 September 2001. http://www.guardian.co.uk/world/2001/sep/26/afghanistan.features11 (accessed August 30, 2010).

Yousafzai, Sami. "Afghanistan Feels the Squeeze." *Newsweek*, January 3, 2011. http://proquest.umi.com.lumen.cgsccarl.com/pqdweb?index=0&did=2229985721&SrchMode=1&sid=2&Fmt=3&VInst=PROD&VType=PQD&RQT=309&VName=PQD&TS=1306037803&clientId=5094 (accessed May 7, 2011).

─────. ─How the Taliban Lost Its Swagger." *Newsweek*, March 7, 2011. http://proquest.umi.com.lumen.cgsccarl.com/pqdweb?index=0&did=2281572621 &SrchMode=1&sid=1&Fmt=3&VInst=PROD&VType=PQD&RQT=309&VNa me=PQD&TS=1306012219&clientId=5094 (accessed May 7, 2011).

─────. ─The Mysterious Mullah Omar." *Newsweek*, March 5, 2007. http://proquest.umi. com.lumen.cgsccarl.com/pqdweb?index=0&did=1222977731&SrchMode=1&sid =4&Fmt=3&VInst=PROD&VType=PQD&RQT=309&VName=PQD&TS=1306 038133&clientId=5094 (accessed May 9, 2011).

─────. ─There's Nothing Going On." *Newsweek*, November 1, 2010. http://proquest. umi.com.lumen.cgsccarl.com/pqdweb?index=10&did=2171727501&SrchMode= 1&sid=7&Fmt=3&VInst=PROD&VType=PQD&RQT=309&VName=PQD&TS =1306038596&clientId=5094 (accessed March 6, 2011).

─────. ─This Mullah Omar Show." *Newsweek*, August 16, 2010. http://proquest.umi. com.lumen.cgsccarl.com/pqdweb?index=25&did=2104847411&SrchMode=1&si d=2&Fmt=3&VInst=PROD&VType=PQD&RQT=309&VName=PQD&TS=130 6012672&clientId=5094 (accessed September 24, 2010).

─────. ─Taliban in Turmoil." *Newsweek*, June 7, 2010. http://proquest.umi.com.lumen. cgsccarl.com/pqdweb?index=0&did=2046681941&SrchMode=1&sid=1&Fmt=1 &VInst=PROD&VType=PQD&RQT=309&VName=PQD&TS=1306037410&cli entId=5094 (accessed March 6, 2011).

Government Documents

Danspeckgruber, Wolfgang. *Petersberg Papers on Afghanistan and the Region.* Vol. 4 of *Liechenstein Colloquium Report.* Princeton: Princeton University, 2009. http://www.ciaonet.org.lumen.cgsccarl.com/wps/lisd/0018577/f_0018577_15903. pdf (accessed September 2, 2010).

U.S. Embassy (Islamabad) Cable. ─Afghanistan: In July 2 Meeting, [Excised] Defends Discriminatory Edicts on Women and Girls, and Controls on NGO's." July 2, 1998. Confidential. http://www.gwu.edu/~nsarchiv/NSAEBB/NSAEBB97/ talib9.pdf (accessed October 22, 2010).

─────. ─Finally, A Talkative Talib: Origins and Membership of the Religious Students' Movement." February 20, 1995. Confidential. http://www.gwu.edu/~nsarchiv/ NSAEBB/NSAEBB97/tal8.pdf (accessed 23 October 2010).

Online Sources

Central Intelligence Agency World Factbook. ─Afghanistan." https://www.cia.gov/ library/publications/the-world-factbook/geos/af.html (accessed May 7, 2011).

Council on Foreign Relations. "The Taliban in Afghanistan." http://www.cfr.org/
  publication/10551/taliban_in_afghanistan.html (accessed October 22, 2010).

Country Watch Afghanistan. "Foreign Relations." http://www.countrywatch.com.lumen.
  cgsccarl.com/cw_topic.aspx?type=text&vcountry=1&topic=POFOR.

Hammond, Andrew. "Islamic Caliphate a Dream, not Reality." *Middle East Online*,
  December 13, 2006. http://www.middle-east-online.com/english/?id=18746
  (accessed May 7, 2011).

Iskra Research. "Maoism versus Marxism." May 1994. http://web.mit.edu/people/
  fjk/essays/maoism.html (accessed November 22, 2010).

Jalili, Ali A. "Wither the Taliban?" Foreign Military Office. 6 March 1999.
  http://fmso.leavenworth.army.mil/documents/taliban.htm (accessed May 8, 2011).

Jane's World Insurgency and Terrorism. "Taliban." http://search.janes.com.lumen.
  cgsccarl.com/Search/documentView.do?docId=/content1/janesdata/binder/jwit/jw
  it0270.htm@current&pageSelected=janesReference&keyword=Taliban&backPat
  h=http://search.janes.com.lumen.cgsccarl.com/Search&Prod_Name=JWIT&
  (accessed October 22, 2010).

Khan, Ehsan Mehmood. "A Strategic Perspective on Taliban Warfare." *Small Wars
  Journal* (2010). http://smallwarsjournal.com/blog/journal/docs-temp/396-
  khan.pdf (accessed September 2, 2010).

The Marxist Archive Site. "The Selected Works of Mao Tse-Tung."
  http://www.marxists.org/reference/archive/mao/index.htm (accessed October 14,
  2010).

The National Security Archive. "The September 11th Sourcebooks." http://www.gwu.
  edu/~nsarchiv/NSAEBB/sept11/ (accessed September 15, 2010).

Nine Eleven Finding Answers (NEFA) Foundation. "Taliban: A Book of Rules."
  September 10, 2009. http://www.nefafoundation.org/miscellaneous/
  nefa_talibancodeconduct.pdf (accessed April 5, 2011).

Program for Culture and Conflict Studies. "The Taliban." Naval Postgraduate School.
  http://www.nps.edu/programs/CCS/Docs/Pubs/The%20Taliban.pdf (accessed
  October 22, 2010).

Visual Sources

Keane, David. *Inside the Taliban.* Directed by David Keane. National Geographic
  Channel, 2007.

Najibullah Quraishi. *Behind Taliban Lines*, Produced by Ken Dornstein. Clover Films, 2010. http://www.pbs.org/wgbh/pages/frontline/talibanlines/ (April 6, 2011).

www.ingramcontent.com/pod-product-compliance
Lightning Source LLC
Chambersburg PA
CBHW081844280526
45789CB00007B/2558